# My First Canadian Atlas

*Written and designed by*

**Nicola Wright • Tony Potter • Christine Wilson • Dee Turner • Chris Leishman**

*Illustrated by*

**Lyn Mitchell**

## Contents

Whitecap Books Ltd.
Vancouver/Toronto

# All about maps

A map is a picture of a place from above. Imagine what your home would look like if you flew over it in an airplane and took a photograph. The picture would show the area around your home spread out flat.

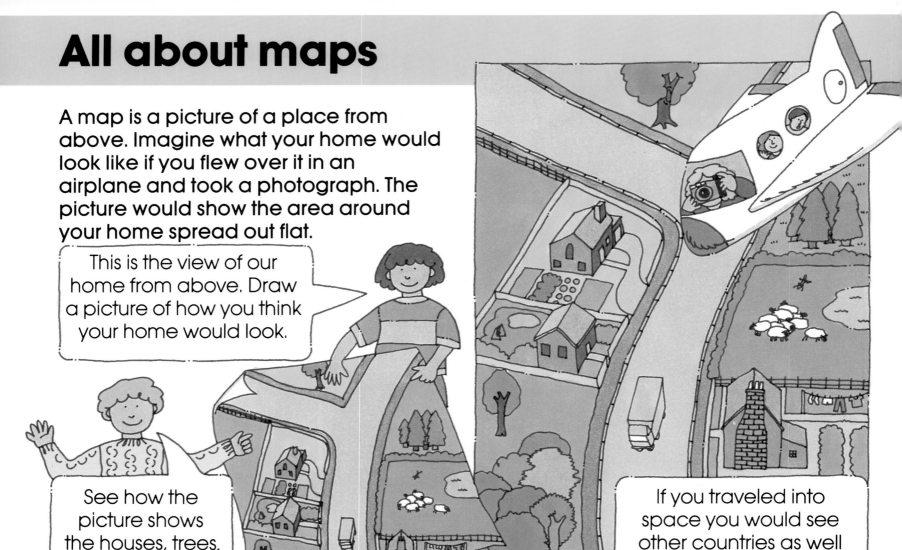

This is the view of our home from above. Draw a picture of how you think your home would look.

See how the picture shows the houses, trees, and roads.

If you traveled into space you would see other countries as well as your island.

**My town**

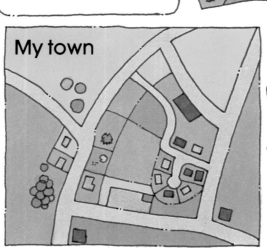

Imagine that you fly higher. Now you can see your whole town or city. Everything looks tiny.

**My island**

Imagine your town is on an island. As you go even higher you can see the whole island.

**The Earth**

Clouds form in the sky and swirl around the Earth. There is much more ocean than land.

This is how my island would look as a map. Tiny pictures called symbols are used to stand for real things.

The pictures below are the symbols used in this book. This part of an atlas is called the **legend**. The legend tells you what the symbols stand for.

Looking for a country? Here is what to do: Go to the list on page 40 and look under the first letter of the country name. So, **Chile** is under the letter **C**.

 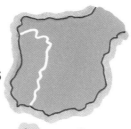 **Country boundaries**

 **Oceans and Seas**

 **Capital cities** ■ Moscow

**Large cities** ● Vladivostok

 **Lakes**

**Rivers**

 **High mountains**

**Low mountains**

 **Tropical rain forest**

 **Monsoon woodland** (hot areas with a rainy season)

 **Pine forest**

 **Leafy woodland**

 **Mixed woodland**

 **Mediterranean woodland** (dry areas with evergreen trees)

 **Desert** (some deserts are just sandy, but some are stony and covered with bushes or cacti)

**Grassland** (called **prairie** in North America, and **pampas** in South America)

**Steppe** (scrubland or grassland in Asia)

 **Savannah** (dry grasslands with some trees in Africa)

**Tundra** (frozen land)

 **Ice**

3

# World map

This big map shows the world as though its round shape has been flattened out. The differently colored areas of land are called continents. There are seven continents and four oceans.

This is planet Earth. Imagine a line around its middle. This is called the equator.

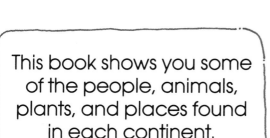

This book shows you some of the people, animals, plants, and places found in each continent.

The biggest continent is Asia. The smallest continent is Australia.

## Countries

The maps in this book show all the countries in the world. A white line shows where one country joins another.

Every country has a flag. Some of them are shown in this book.

The Polish flag

The Belgian flag

Portugal

The Italian flag

Arctic Ocean

North America

Atlantic Ocean

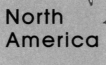

Equator

Pacific Ocean

South America

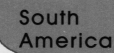

Atlantic Ocean

The bottom half of the world is called the southern hemisphere.

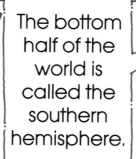

SOUTH POLE

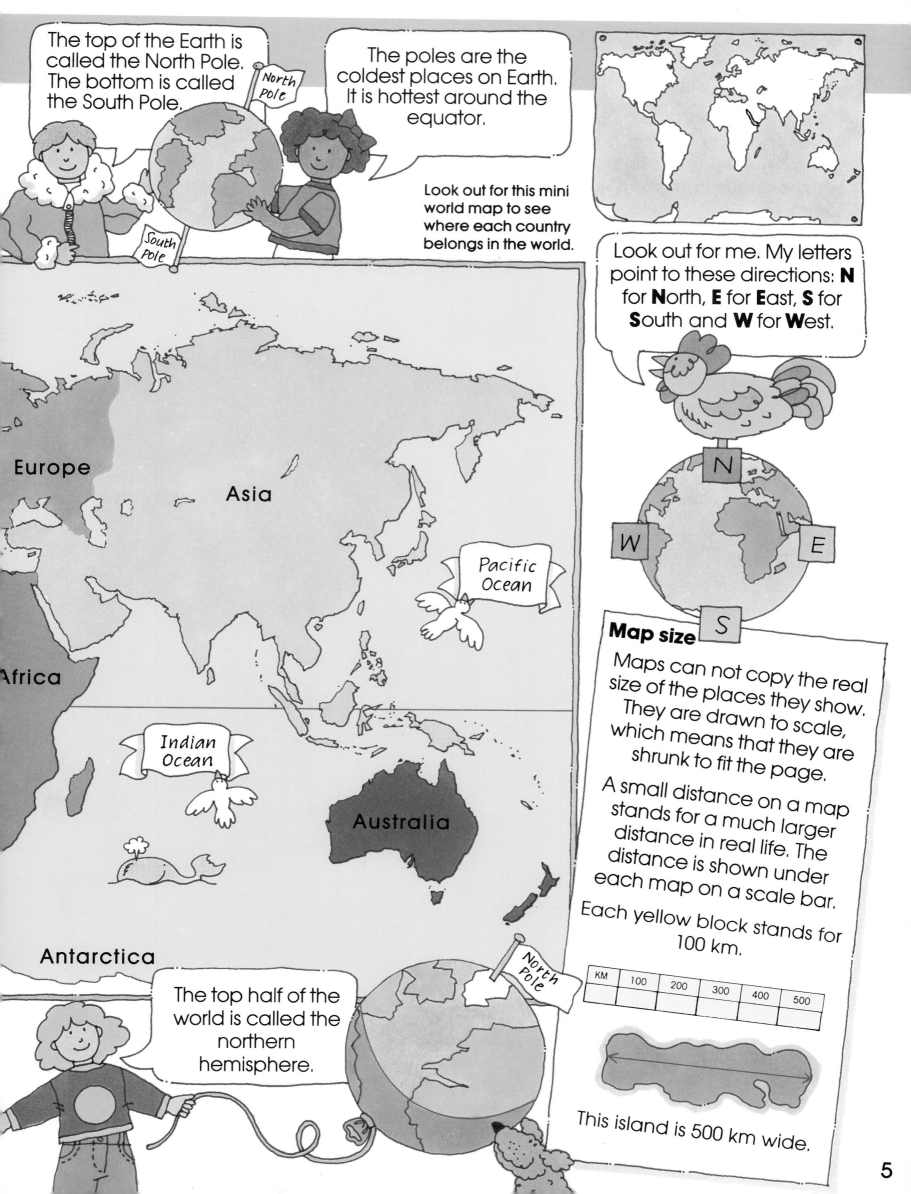

The top of the Earth is called the North Pole. The bottom is called the South Pole.

North Pole

South Pole

The poles are the coldest places on Earth. It is hottest around the equator.

Look out for this mini world map to see where each country belongs in the world.

Look out for me. My letters point to these directions: **N** for **N**orth, **E** for **E**ast, **S** for **S**outh and **W** for **W**est.

N

W

E

S

Europe

Asia

Africa

Pacific Ocean

Indian Ocean

Australia

Antarctica

**Map size**

Maps can not copy the real size of the places they show. They are drawn to scale, which means that they are shrunk to fit the page.

A small distance on a map stands for a much larger distance in real life. The distance is shown under each map on a scale bar.

Each yellow block stands for 100 km.

| KM | 100 | 200 | 300 | 400 | 500 |
|----|-----|-----|-----|-----|-----|

This island is 500 km wide.

The top half of the world is called the northern hemisphere.

North Pole

5

# Canada

**Canada is the second largest country in the world. It is divided into ten provinces and two territories. Each province and territory has a capital city. On the map, these capitals are marked with a small star. Ottawa, the capital city of Canada, is marked with a large star. About 27 million people live in Canada.**

Canada's vast northern territories – Yukon and the Northwest Territories – extend far to the north. Few people live in the far north.

The Rocky Mountains form what is called the Continental Divide. Rivers run down one side of the Rockies to the Pacific Ocean, and down the other side to the Arctic and Atlantic oceans.

Pacific Ocean

Mackenzie River

Great Bear Lake

**YUKON**
★ WHITEHORSE

**NORTHWEST TERRITORIES**

YELLOWKNIFE ★

Great Slave Lake

C A N A

Rocky

Peace River

Lake Athabasca

Prince Rupert

**ALBERTA**

**SASKATCHEWAN**

**MANITOB**

Lake Winnipeg

**BRITISH COLUMBIA**

Mountains

EDMONTON ★

Vancouver

Calgary

Saskatoon

VICTORIA

REGINA ★

WINNIPEG

Manitoba, Saskatchewan and Alberta are called the Prairie Provinces. Much of these provinces is flat and good for farming.

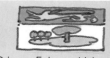
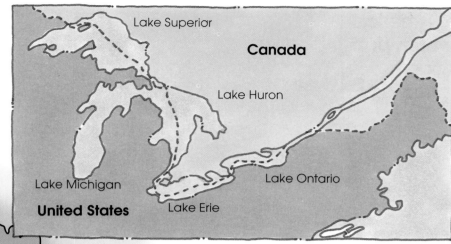

The Great Lakes are big lakes along the boundary of Ontario and the United States. The lakes are connected to the Atlantic Ocean by the St. Lawrence Seaway and river.

Newfoundland was the first part of Canada explored by European sailors. The province has two parts – the island of Newfoundland and Labrador on the mainland.

Nova Scotia, New Brunswick and Prince Edward Island are the Maritime Provinces.

Québec is the largest province. Most people who live here speak French. English and French are the official languages of Canada.

Ontario is the second largest province. More people live in Ontario than any other province – over 10 million.

7

# The story of Canada

Canada's first people came to North America across the northern part of the continent thousands of years ago.

## 1497

British explorer John Cabot claimed Newfoundland for England. Viking explorers had been to Newfoundland as early as the 1100s.

## 1534, 1535 and 1541

During three voyages of exploration for France, Jacques Cartier drew maps of the St. Lawrence area and named it Canada.

## 1603-1632

Samuel de Champlain helped establish colonies at today's Québec City, and Port-Royal in Nova Scotia.

## 1791

Most of the early settlers lived along the St. Lawrence River. "Upper Canada" was up the river from "Lower Canada." Upper and Lower Canada were the beginnings of today's provinces of Ontario and Québec.

Settlers followed the early explorers. They began to clear the land and farm it.

Coureurs de bois – runners of the woods – travelled on rivers and lakes in canoes made of birch bark. They bought valuable furs from native people. Fur traders were the first Europeans to explore much of inland Canada.

## 1792

Captain George Vancouver came to the coast of British Columbia. While the east coast of Canada was being settled by Europeans, the west coast was just beginning to be explored.

On July 1, 1867, the colonies of New Brunswick, Nova Scotia, Ontario and Québec joined together to form the Dominion of Canada. Sir John A. Macdonald was the first prime minister.

**1876**

The first long-distance telephone call in the world took place in Paris, Ontario. Alexander Graham Bell, inventor of the telephone, called his uncle in Brantford, Ontario.

**1880**

By 1880, the Dominion of Canada included all of today's Canada, except for Newfoundland, which joined in 1949.

**1885**

The last spike in the Canadian Pacific Railway was pounded in at Craigellachie, in British Columbia. This important railway linked the settlements, which were few and far apart.

**1896**

Gold was discovered on the Klondike River in the Yukon. Prospectors rushed in from all over the world.

**1922**

Dr. Frederick Banting discovered that insulin could control diabetes. He received a Nobel Prize for his work.

**1981**

Canadian scientists developed a special robot arm, called the Canadarm, for the U.S. Space Shuttle. It is 15 metres long and can pick up and repair satellites in space.

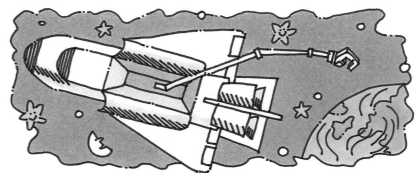

# Things to See

Niagara Falls, in Ontario, are 675 metres wide – about as wide as five city blocks.

British Columbia's Queen Charlotte Islands are called Haida Gwaii by the native Haida people. There you can see tall poles, beautifully painted and carved by Haida artists.

The Rockies have some of the highest mountains in Canada.

You can ride in a horse–drawn carriage around the beautiful city of Québec.

Prince Edward Island is the setting for Anne of Green Gables, a story written by Lucy Maud Montgomery in 1908. Visitors come from all over the world to see the cottage used as the model for Green Gables.

Many dinosaur bones have been found in the Badlands area of southern Alberta, near Drumheller. You can see real fossils and life-size replicas of these huge extinct animals.

The CN Tower in Toronto is 553 metres high – the highest free-standing structure in the world.

# What people do

The flat prairies have rich soil that is good for growing wheat and other grains.

"Bush pilots" fly small airplanes that take people into remote parts of Canada.

Apples, cherries, peaches and grapes are grown in the Okanagan Valley, in British Columbia, and the southern parts of Ontario.

In Alberta, there are many cattle ranches. There are also ranches in the interior of British Columbia.

Miners remove ore, such as iron, copper, coal, gold, zinc, nickel and silver from Canada's rocky areas.

Forestry is an important industry in Canada. The trees are used for both lumber and paper.

Salmon, cod, lobster, shrimp and crab are among the seafood caught on the Atlantic and Pacific coasts.

Prince Edward Island is famous for its potato crops. It is sometimes called Spud Island.

Canada's great natural beauty attracts a lot of travellers. Many people work in hotels and restaurants, or as guides to out-of-the-way places.

# Wildlife

Canada has huge areas where few people live, so there are many animals.

Canada geese fly in V-shaped formations. They are the most common geese in Canada.

The bald eagle is usually found near water. It builds its huge nest high in a tree. The nest can be up to 3 metres across and weigh as much as a small car.

Deer are found all across Canada. In the spring the fawns are born.

Prairie dogs and gophers live mostly underground, where they dig complex tunnels. Mounds of dirt mark the entrances to their burrows.

Wolves are found mainly in Canada's north.

The prairies were once the home of herds of bison numbering in the millions. Today small herds are protected in four parks.

Raccoons live across most of southern Canada, even in the cities. Their black face markings look like a mask.

A male moose grows a set of antlers, called a "rack." Each year, until it is about ten, a moose's rack grows larger.

Barrenground caribou are great travellers. Each year they migrate across the Arctic along trails they have followed for centuries.

Canada has many bears. Black bears live in the forests across Canada. Grizzlies are huge bears that occupy more remote regions. The polar bear lives in the far north.

Seals, like whales, are marine mammals. You can often see harbour seals around docks and shorelines.

Killer whales, or orcas, have beautiful black and white markings. They are often seen on the Pacific and Atlantic coasts. They usually travel in family groups called pods.

Beluga whales are completely white. Large amounts of blubber help them survive in the cold Arctic waters where they live.

# North America

North America contains Canada, the United States of America, Mexico, and the countries of Central America. Canada is the second largest country in the world. The U.S. is the fourth largest and has fifty states.

*The Canadian flag*

Ice hockey is a very popular sport in Canada.

Skiing is popular in the Rocky mountains. The Rockies run from Canada, through the United States.

The U.S. produces more timber than any other country.

Canadian police are called Mounties. Some still ride horses, but most drive cars or motorcycles nowadays

One of the world's most active volcanos, Mauna Loa, is in Hawaii.

**Hawaii (USA)**

The Aztecs were a civilization in Mexico hundreds of years ago. Mexicans are proud of their Aztec ancestry.

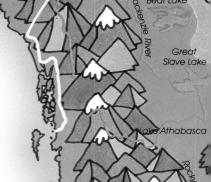

**Alaska (USA)**

*Yukon River*

*Alaskan Mountains*

Fairbanks •

• Anchorage

*Great Bear Lake*

*Mackenzie River*

*Great Slave Lake*

*Lake Athabasca*

*Rocky Mountains*

Vancouver •

*Columbia River*

*Snake River*

*Sierra Nevada*

*Coastal Mountains*

Los Angeles
San Diego

*Colorado River*

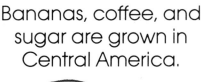
*The American flag*

*Pacific Ocean*

Bananas, coffee, and sugar are grown in Central America.

*The Mexican flag*

## Fact file

 *Highest mountain:* Mount Mckinley, Alaska, 6,194 m.

*Longest river:* Mississippi-Missouri River, U.S., 6,212 km.

*Largest lake:* Lake Superior, U.S.-Canada, is the second largest in the world. 82,383 sq km.

*Weather:* Canada and Alaska are colder than the rest of North America.

*Biggest city:* Mexico City, Mexico, about 9 million people.

*Number of people:* Canada, about 30 million. U.S., about 256 million. Mexico, about 86 million. Costa Rica, about 3 million. Panama, about 3 million.

| KM | 250 | 500 | 1000 | 1500 | 2000 | 2500 | 3000 | 3500 | 4000 | 4500 | 5000 | 5500 | 6000 | 650 |
|---|---|---|---|---|---|---|---|---|---|---|---|---|---|---|
| | | | | | | | | | | | | | | |

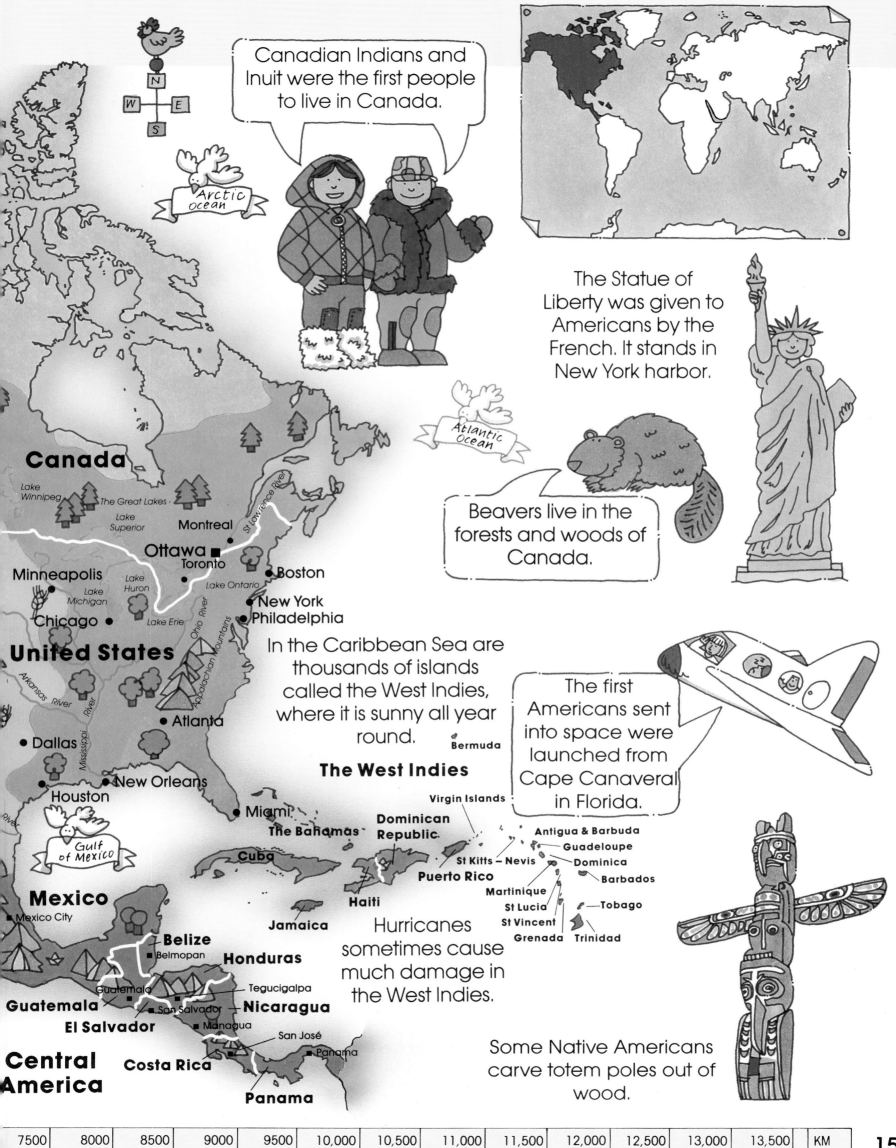

Canadian Indians and Inuit were the first people to live in Canada.

Arctic ocean

The Statue of Liberty was given to Americans by the French. It stands in New York harbor.

Atlantic Ocean

Beavers live in the forests and woods of Canada.

**Canada**

Lake Winnipeg

The Great Lakes -

Lake Superior

Lake Michigan

Lake Huron

Lake Erie

Lake Ontario

Montreal

St Lawrence River

Ottawa

Toronto

Boston

Minneapolis

New York

Philadelphia

Chicago

Ohio River

Appalachian Mountains

**United States**

Arkansas River

Mississippi River

Atlanta

Dallas

New Orleans

Houston

Gulf of Mexico

Miami

In the Caribbean Sea are thousands of islands called the West Indies, where it is sunny all year round.

Bermuda

**The West Indies**

Virgin Islands

**The Bahamas**

**Dominican Republic**

**Cuba**

**Puerto Rico**

**Haiti**

**Jamaica**

Antigua & Barbuda

Guadeloupe

St Kitts – Nevis

Dominica

Barbados

Martinique

St Lucia

Tobago

St Vincent

Grenada   Trinidad

The first Americans sent into space were launched from Cape Canaveral in Florida.

**Mexico**

Mexico City

**Belize**

Belmopan

**Honduras**

**Guatemala**

Guatemala

Tegucigalpa

San Salvador

**Nicaragua**

**El Salvador**

Managua

San José

**Central America**

**Costa Rica**

Panama

**Panama**

Hurricanes sometimes cause much damage in the West Indies.

Some Native Americans carve totem poles out of wood.

| 7500 | 8000 | 8500 | 9000 | 9500 | 10,000 | 10,500 | 11,000 | 11,500 | 12,000 | 12,500 | 13,000 | 13,500 | KM |
|------|------|------|------|------|--------|--------|--------|--------|--------|--------|--------|--------|-----|

# South America

South America is the fourth largest continent. It is made up of 13 different countries. There are mountains and rain forests as well as plains and deserts. The weather ranges from very hot to very cold.

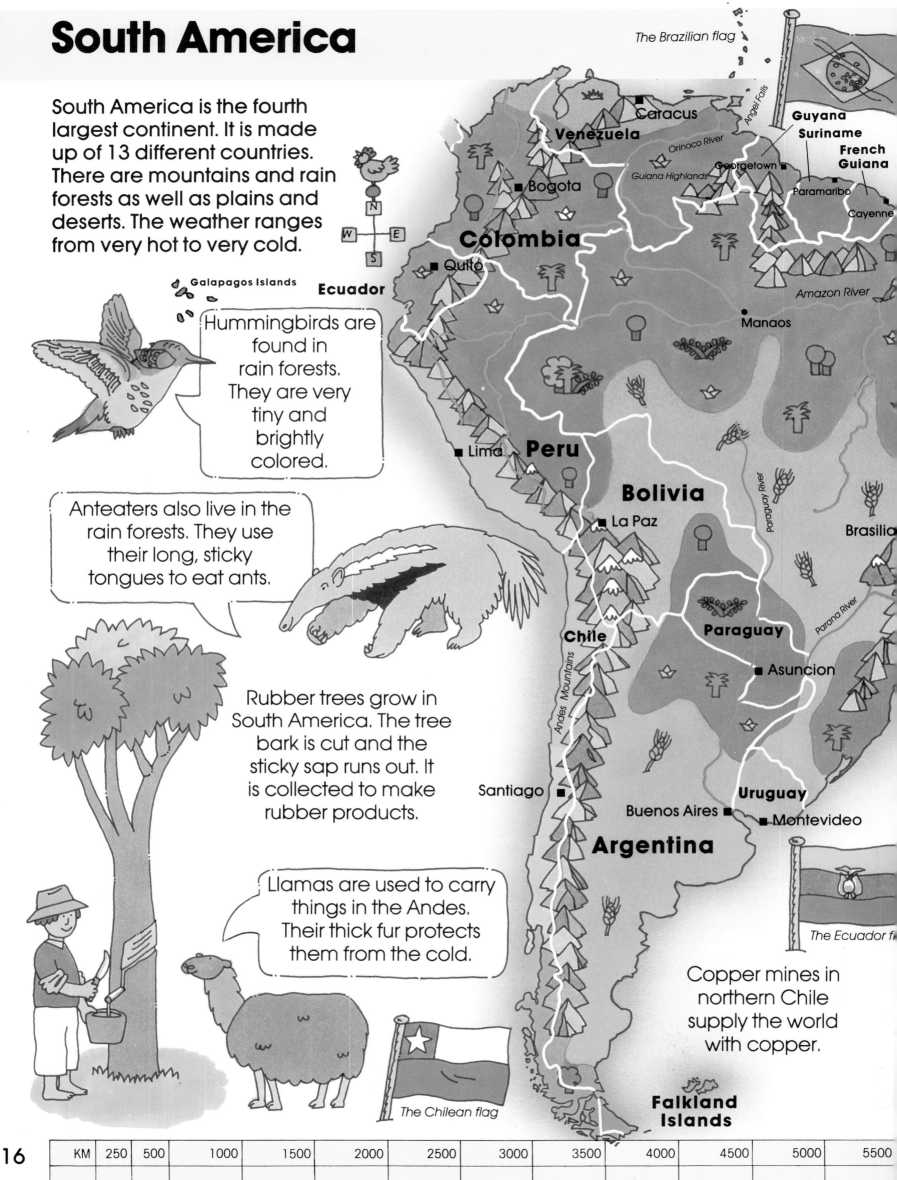

Hummingbirds are found in rain forests. They are very tiny and brightly colored.

Anteaters also live in the rain forests. They use their long, sticky tongues to eat ants.

Rubber trees grow in South America. The tree bark is cut and the sticky sap runs out. It is collected to make rubber products.

Llamas are used to carry things in the Andes. Their thick fur protects them from the cold.

Copper mines in northern Chile supply the world with copper.

The Brazilian flag

Galapagos Islands

Ecuador

Venezuela
Caracus
Bogota
Colombia
Quito

Orinoco River
Guiana Highlands
Georgetown
Paramaribo
Cayenne

Guyana
Suriname
French Guiana

Angel Falls

Amazon River
Manaos

Lima
Peru

Bolivia
La Paz

Paraguay River
Brasilia

Chile
Andes Mountains

Paraguay
Asuncion

Parana River

Santiago

Uruguay
Buenos Aires
Montevideo

Argentina

The Ecuador f

The Chilean flag

Falkland Islands

| KM | 250 | 500 | 1000 | 1500 | 2000 | 2500 | 3000 | 3500 | 4000 | 4500 | 5000 | 5500 |
|----|-----|-----|------|------|------|------|------|------|------|------|------|------|
|    |     |     |      |      |      |      |      |      |      |      |      |      |

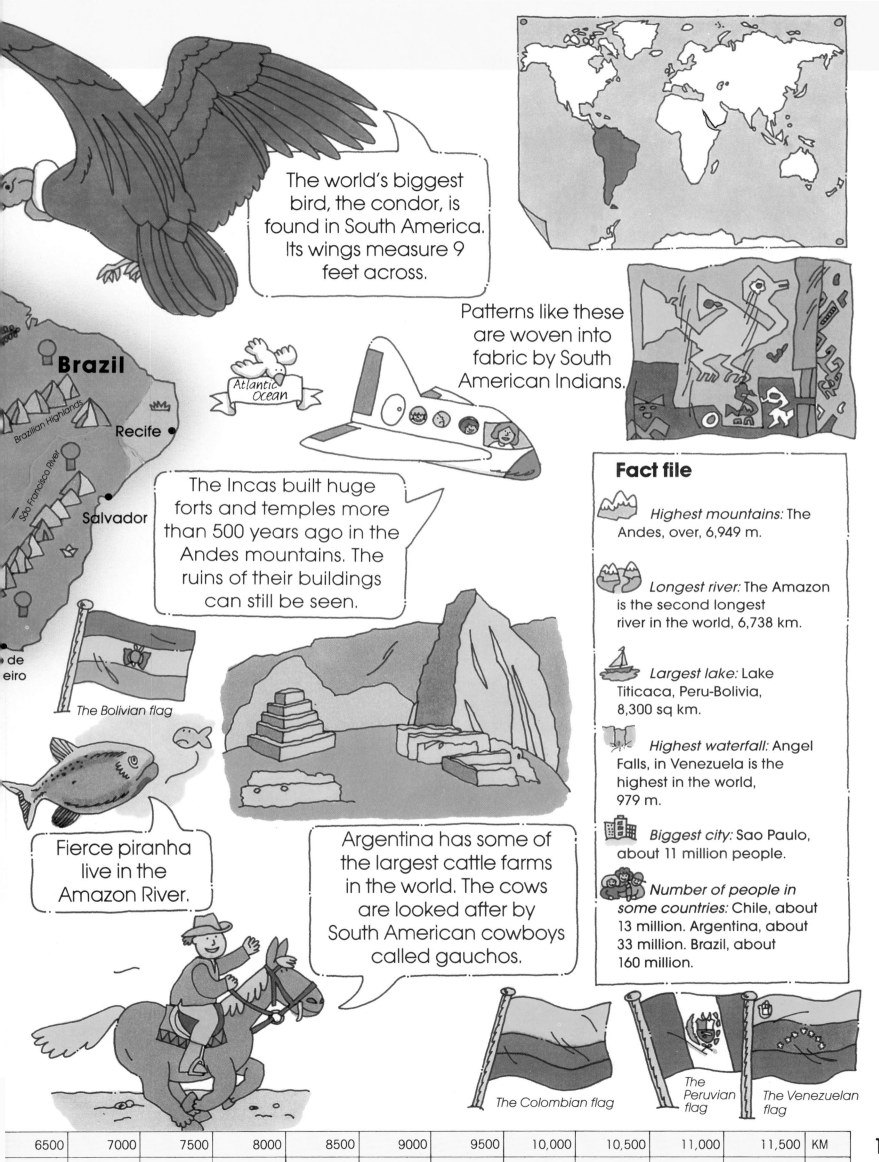

The world's biggest bird, the condor, is found in South America. Its wings measure 9 feet across.

Patterns like these are woven into fabric by South American Indians.

**Brazil**

Brazilian Highlands

Recife •

São Francisco River

Salvador •

Atlantic Ocean

The Incas built huge forts and temples more than 500 years ago in the Andes mountains. The ruins of their buildings can still be seen.

de eiro

The Bolivian flag

Fierce piranha live in the Amazon River.

Argentina has some of the largest cattle farms in the world. The cows are looked after by South American cowboys called gauchos.

### Fact file

*Highest mountains:* The Andes, over, 6,949 m.

*Longest river:* The Amazon is the second longest river in the world, 6,738 km.

*Largest lake:* Lake Titicaca, Peru-Bolivia, 8,300 sq km.

*Highest waterfall:* Angel Falls, in Venezuela is the highest in the world, 979 m.

*Biggest city:* Sao Paulo, about 11 million people.

*Number of people in some countries:* Chile, about 13 million. Argentina, about 33 million. Brazil, about 160 million.

The Colombian flag

The Peruvian flag

The Venezuelan flag

| 6500 | 7000 | 7500 | 8000 | 8500 | 9000 | 9500 | 10,000 | 10,500 | 11,000 | 11,500 | KM |
|------|------|------|------|------|------|------|--------|--------|--------|--------|-----|
| | | | | | | | | | | | |

# Northern Europe

These northern European countries are known as Scandinavia. Norway has over 150,000 islands along its coastline. The Norwegian coast is jagged, with deep inlets called fjords. Forests and lakes cover large areas of Scandinavia. Many bears and wolves used to live in the forests.

Workers travel to the oil rigs by helicopter.

There is oil under the sea bed. Oil rigs are used to pump the oil up to the surface.

Children here learn to ski almost as soon as they can walk!

The oil is used as fuel for cars and for heating buildings.

Trawlers are fishing boats that catch fish by dragging nets along the sea bed. Many Norwegian fishing boats fish in the North Sea.

Some fishing boats can stay out at sea for months at a time.

*The Danish flag*

*The Norwegian flag*

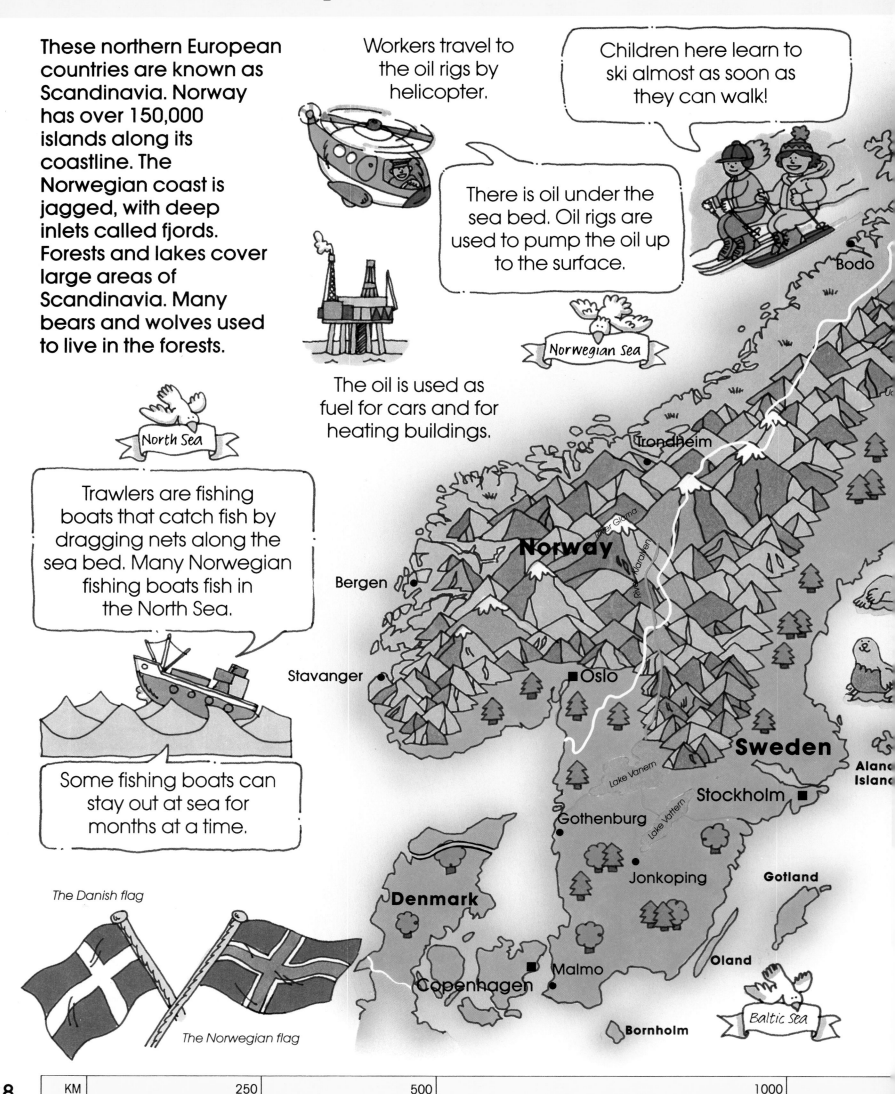

North Sea

Norwegian Sea

Bodo

Trondheim

River Glama

Norway

Bergen

River Klaralven

Stavanger

Oslo

Sweden

Lake Vanern

Alan Island

Stockholm

Gothenburg

Lake Vattern

Jonkoping

Gotland

Denmark

Oland

Malmo

Copenhagen

Bornholm

Baltic Sea

| KM | 250 | 500 | 1000 |
|---|---|---|---|
| | | | |

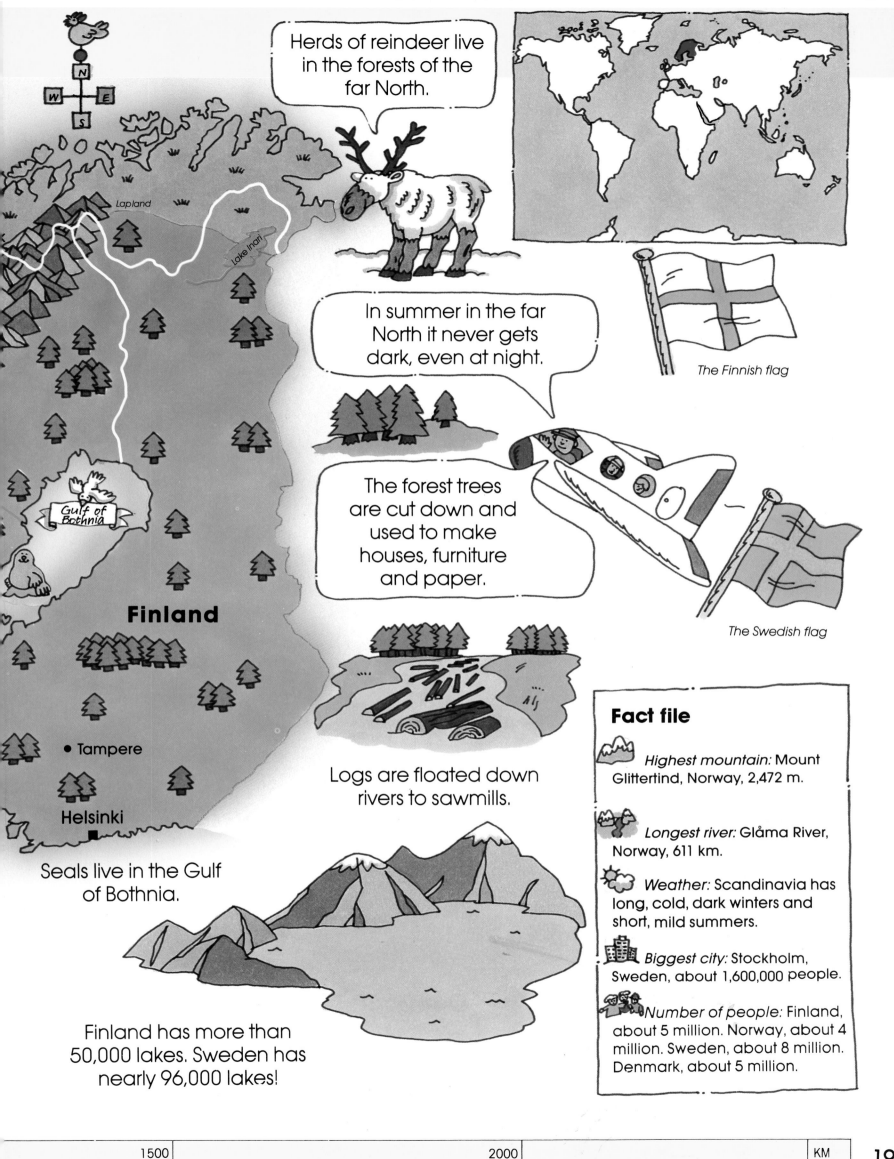

Herds of reindeer live in the forests of the far North.

In summer in the far North it never gets dark, even at night.

The forest trees are cut down and used to make houses, furniture and paper.

The Finnish flag

The Swedish flag

**Finland**

Lapland

Lake Inari

Gulf of Bothnia

• Tampere

Helsinki

Logs are floated down rivers to sawmills.

Seals live in the Gulf of Bothnia.

Finland has more than 50,000 lakes. Sweden has nearly 96,000 lakes!

**Fact file**

*Highest mountain:* Mount Glittertind, Norway, 2,472 m.

*Longest river:* Glåma River, Norway, 611 km.

*Weather:* Scandinavia has long, cold, dark winters and short, mild summers.

*Biggest city:* Stockholm, Sweden, about 1,600,000 people.

*Number of people:* Finland, about 5 million. Norway, about 4 million. Sweden, about 8 million. Denmark, about 5 million.

# Britain and Central Europe

On this map you can see seventeen different countries. Some, like Luxembourg, are tiny. Others, such as France, are large. There are very high mountains, called the Alps, in Switzerland, France, and Austria, but most of the rest of Europe is flatter. The flat land is very good for farming.

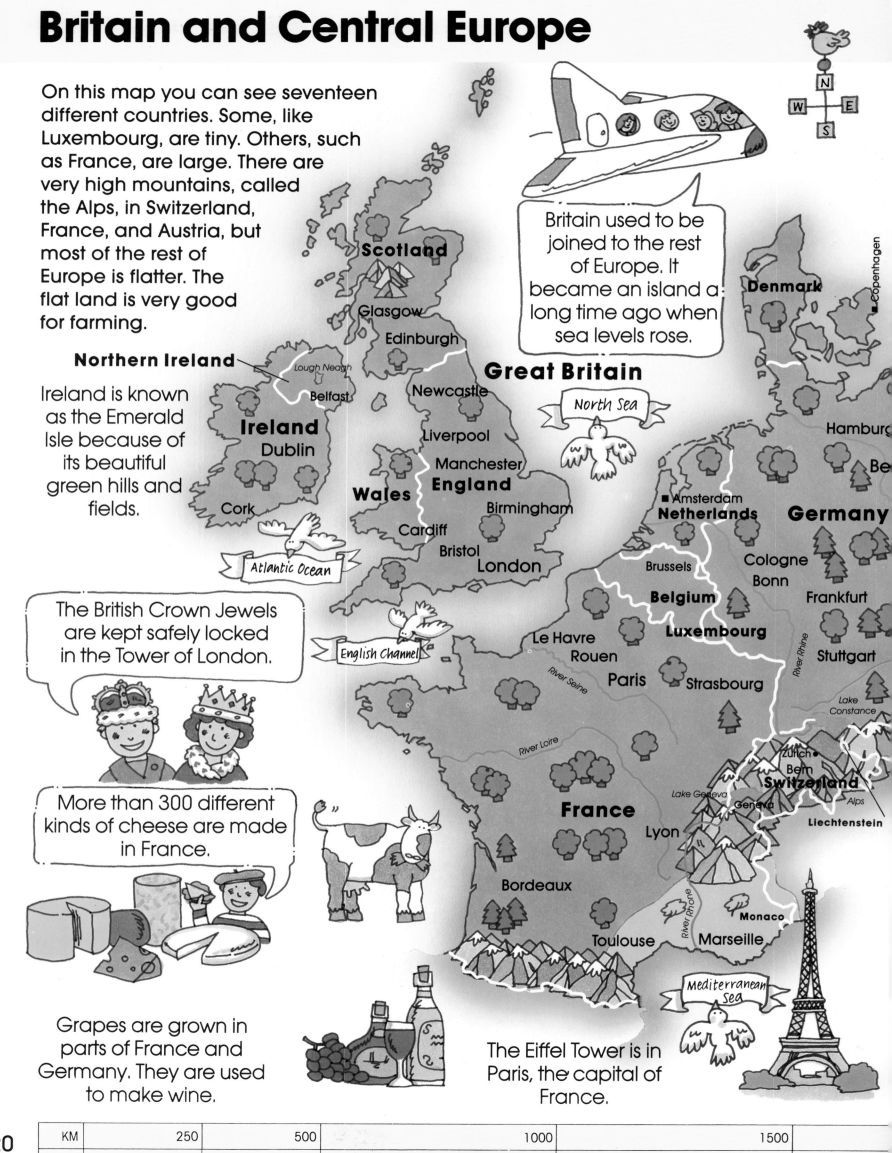

Britain used to be joined to the rest of Europe. It became an island a long time ago when sea levels rose.

**Northern Ireland**

Ireland is known as the Emerald Isle because of its beautiful green hills and fields.

The British Crown Jewels are kept safely locked in the Tower of London.

More than 300 different kinds of cheese are made in France.

Grapes are grown in parts of France and Germany. They are used to make wine.

The Eiffel Tower is in Paris, the capital of France.

Scotland
Glasgow
Edinburgh
Lough Neagh
Belfast
Newcastle
Ireland
Dublin
Liverpool
Manchester
England
Wales
Cork
Cardiff
Birmingham
Bristol
London
Great Britain
North Sea
Denmark
Copenhagen
Hamburg
Amsterdam
Netherlands
Brussels
Belgium
Germany
Cologne
Bonn
Frankfurt
Luxembourg
River Rhine
Stuttgart
Atlantic Ocean
English Channel
Le Havre
Rouen
River Seine
Paris
Strasbourg
Lake Constance
River Loire
France
Lyon
Zurich
Bern
Switzerland
Lake Geneva
Geneva
Alps
Liechtenstein
Bordeaux
Toulouse
River Rhone
Monaco
Marseille
Mediterranean Sea

| | | KM | 250 | 500 | | 1000 | 1500 |
|---|---|---|---|---|---|---|---|
| | | | | | | | |

The Netherlands are so low and flat that the sea can flood in. Sea walls protect the land and windmills pump water away. Many Dutch farmers grow flowers.

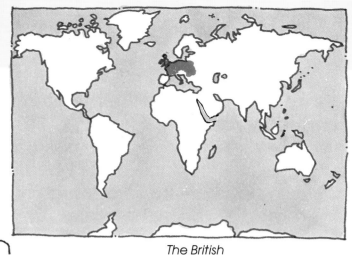

Germany, France, and Britain have big factories making many things from cars to computers.

*The Swiss flag*  *The British Union Jack*  *The French flag*

*The German flag*  *The Austrian flag*

Gdansk

*River Vistula*

Warsaw

Poznan

**Poland**

*River Oder*

Wroclaw

*River Elbe*

Krakow

*Carpathians*

**Czech Republic**  **Slovakia**

Vienna

Bratislava

Budapest

**Hungary**

*River Danube*

*Salzburg*

**Austria**

Cluj-Napoca

**Romania**

Timisoara

Constanta

Bucharest

**Bulgaria**

Sofia

## Fact file

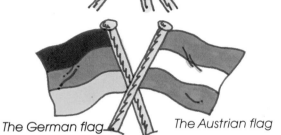 *Highest mountain:* Mont Blanc, France, 4,801 m.

*Longest river:* The Danube, 2,858 km.

*Weather:* Most of this part of Europe has mild winters and cool summers. Rain falls all year round. Snow falls in many places in winter.

*Biggest city:* Paris, France, about 10 million people.

*Number of people in some European countries:* France, about 56 million. Great Britain (England, Scotland and Wales), about 57 million. Germany, about 79 million. Netherlands, about 15 million. Luxembourg, about 378,000.

Skiing is a popular sport in the mountains.

There are many fairytale castles built along the banks of the Rhine River in Germany.

# Mediterranean Europe

The countries around the Mediterranean Sea are sunny all year. Olives, fruit, and vegetables are grown in all these countries. Many people go to the Mediterranean for vacations. In parts of Spain and Italy there are high mountains where people ski in the winter.

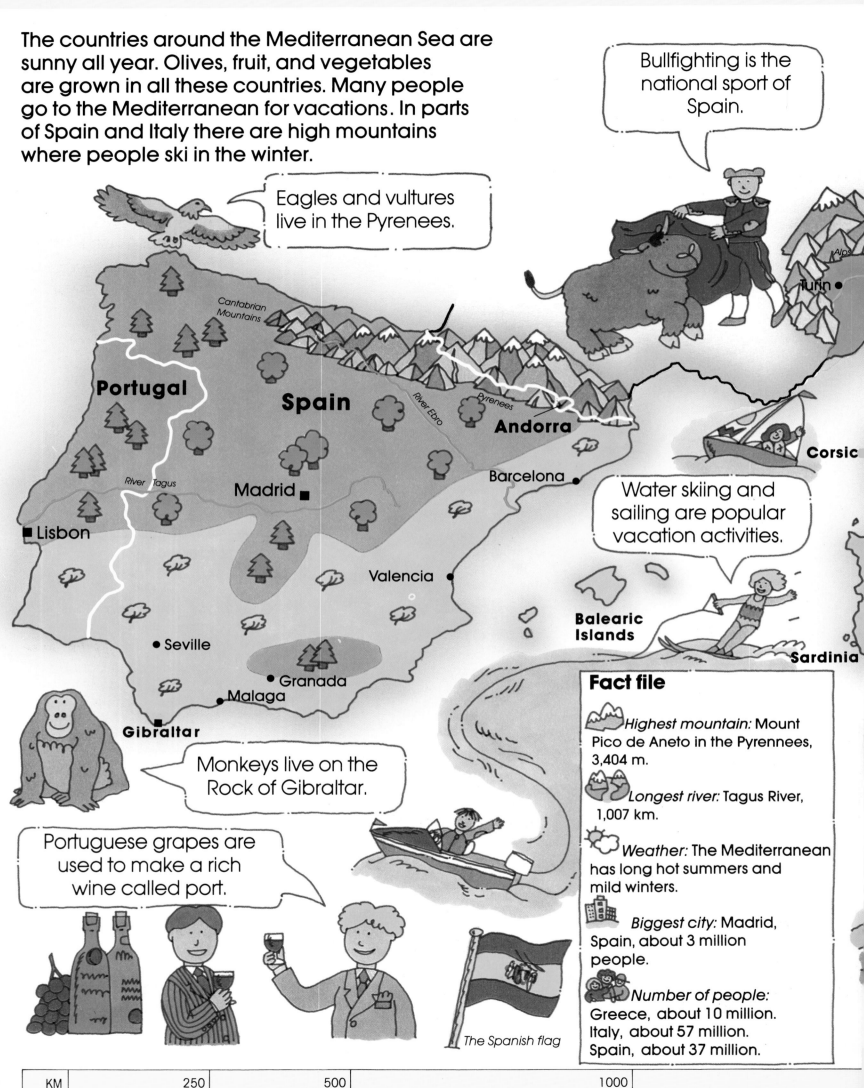

Bullfighting is the national sport of Spain.

Eagles and vultures live in the Pyrenees.

Portugal

Spain

Cantabrian Mountains

River Ebro

Pyrenees

Andorra

Barcelona

Madrid

River Tagus

Lisbon

Valencia

Seville

Granada

Malaga

Gibraltar

Turin

Alps

Corsica

Water skiing and sailing are popular vacation activities.

Balearic Islands

Sardinia

Monkeys live on the Rock of Gibraltar.

Portuguese grapes are used to make a rich wine called port.

The Spanish flag

**Fact file**

*Highest mountain:* Mount Pico de Aneto in the Pyrennees, 3,404 m.

*Longest river:* Tagus River, 1,007 km.

*Weather:* The Mediterranean has long hot summers and mild winters.

*Biggest city:* Madrid, Spain, about 3 million people.

*Number of people:* Greece, about 10 million. Italy, about 57 million. Spain, about 37 million.

| KM | 250 | 500 | 1000 |
|---|---|---|---|

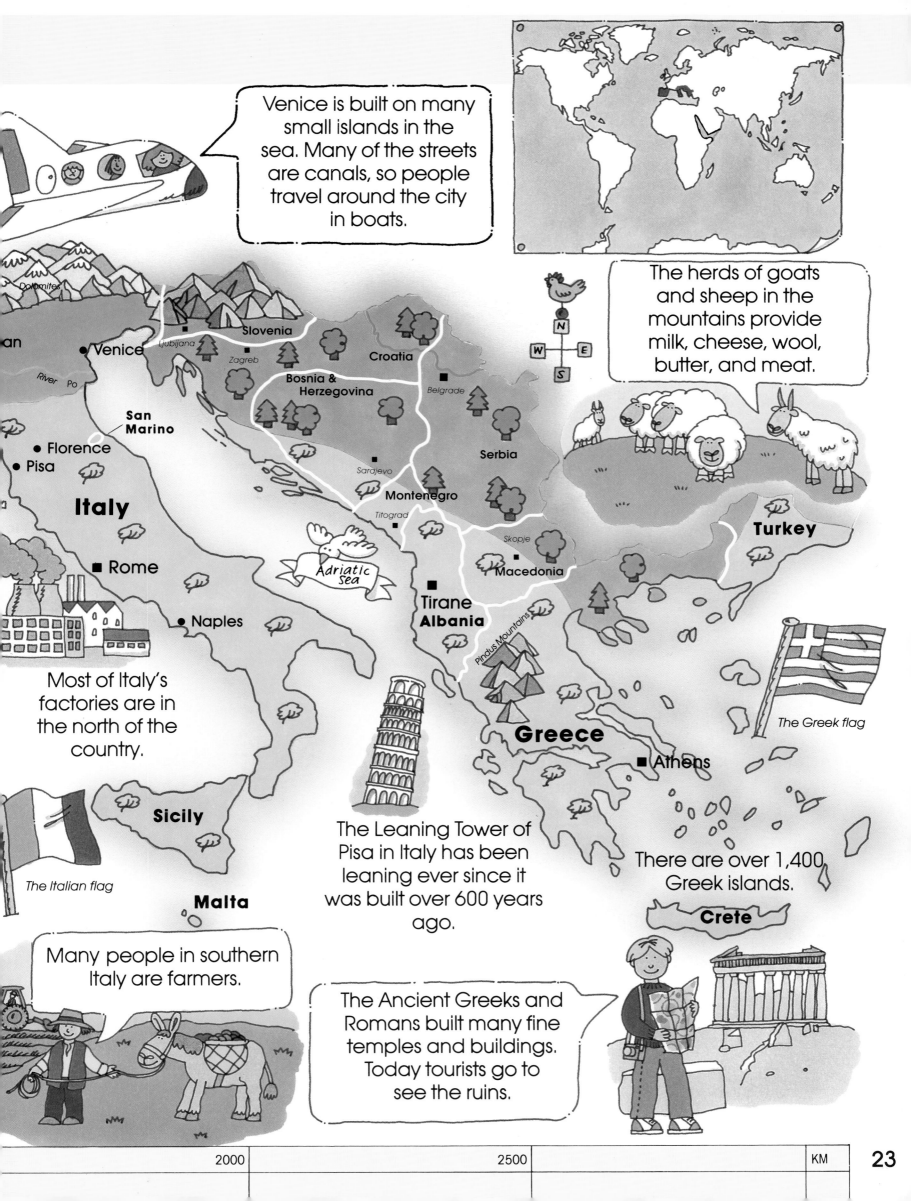

Venice is built on many small islands in the sea. Many of the streets are canals, so people travel around the city in boats.

The herds of goats and sheep in the mountains provide milk, cheese, wool, butter, and meat.

Dolomites

Slovenia
Ljubijana
Zagreb
Croatia
Belgrade
Venice
River Po
Bosnia & Herzegovina
San Marino
Florence
Pisa
Italy
Sarajevo
Serbia
Montenegro
Titograd
Rome
Adriatic Sea
Skopje
Macedonia
Turkey
Naples
Tirane
Albania
Pindus Mountains

Most of Italy's factories are in the north of the country.

Greece

The Greek flag

Athens

Sicily

The Leaning Tower of Pisa in Italy has been leaning ever since it was built over 600 years ago.

There are over 1,400 Greek islands.

The Italian flag

Malta

Crete

Many people in southern Italy are farmers.

The Ancient Greeks and Romans built many fine temples and buildings. Today tourists go to see the ruins.

2000          2500          KM

# Africa

Africa is the second largest continent in the world. It is split up into lots of different countries. Most of Africa is covered in grassland and desert. Some of the tropical rain forests in Africa have been chopped down to build villages and farms.

Cape Verde Islands

Madeira Island (Portugal)

Canary Islands (Spain)

Rabat
Morocco

Algiers
Tunis
Tunisia

The Chad flag

Tripoli

Libya

Atlas Mountains

Western Sahara

Algeria

Mauritania

Nouakchott

Mali

River Niger

Hoggar Mountains

Tibesti Mountains

Niger

Chad

Lake Chad

N'Djamena

Sud

Dakar
Senegal
Banjul
Gambia
Bissau
Guinea-Bissau

Bamako

Burkina Faso
Ouagadougou

Niamey

Guinea
Conakry

Freetown
Sierra Leone

Monrovia

Liberia

Ivory Coast

Ghana

Abidjan

Accra

Benin
Togo

Lomé
Porto-Novo

Nigeria

Abuja

Central African Republic

Cameroon

Bangui

Yaoundé

Equatorial Guinea

Libreville

Congo

Gabon

River Zaire

Zaire

Rwa

Brazzaville

Kinshasa

Bur

All sorts of wild animals are kept in huge safari parks so that they can be protected from danger. Tourists visit the parks.

The Nigerian flag

The African elephant is the largest land animal in the world. Its ear is the same shape as the continent of Africa.

Angola

Luanda

Atlantic Ocean

Angola

Zamb

Lusak

Zambezi River

Diamonds and gold are mined in South Africa.

Namibia

Windhoek

Botswana

Gaborone

Pretoria

Johannesburg

Drakensberg Mountains

Orange River

M

South Africa

Cape Town

Les

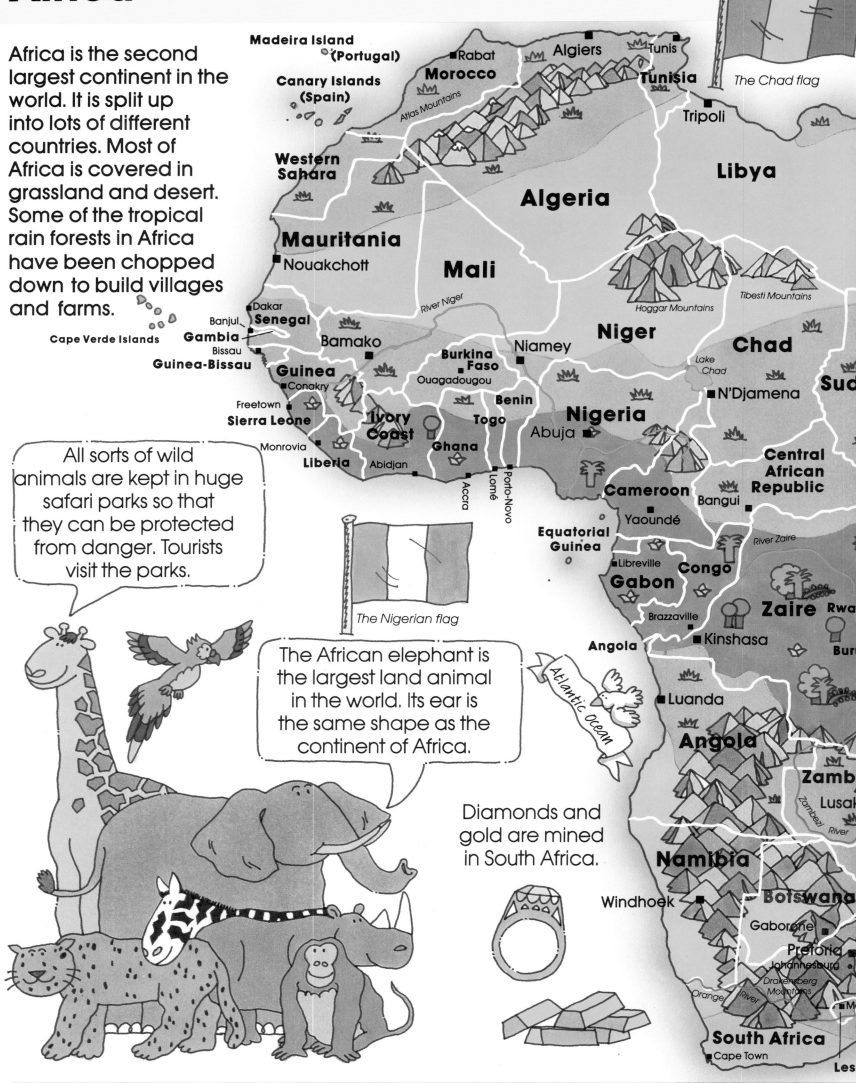

| KM | 250 | 500 | 1000 | 1500 | 2000 | 2500 | 3000 | 3500 | 4000 | 4500 | 5000 | 5500 | 6000 | 6500 |
|---|---|---|---|---|---|---|---|---|---|---|---|---|---|---|
| | | | | | | | | | | | | | | |

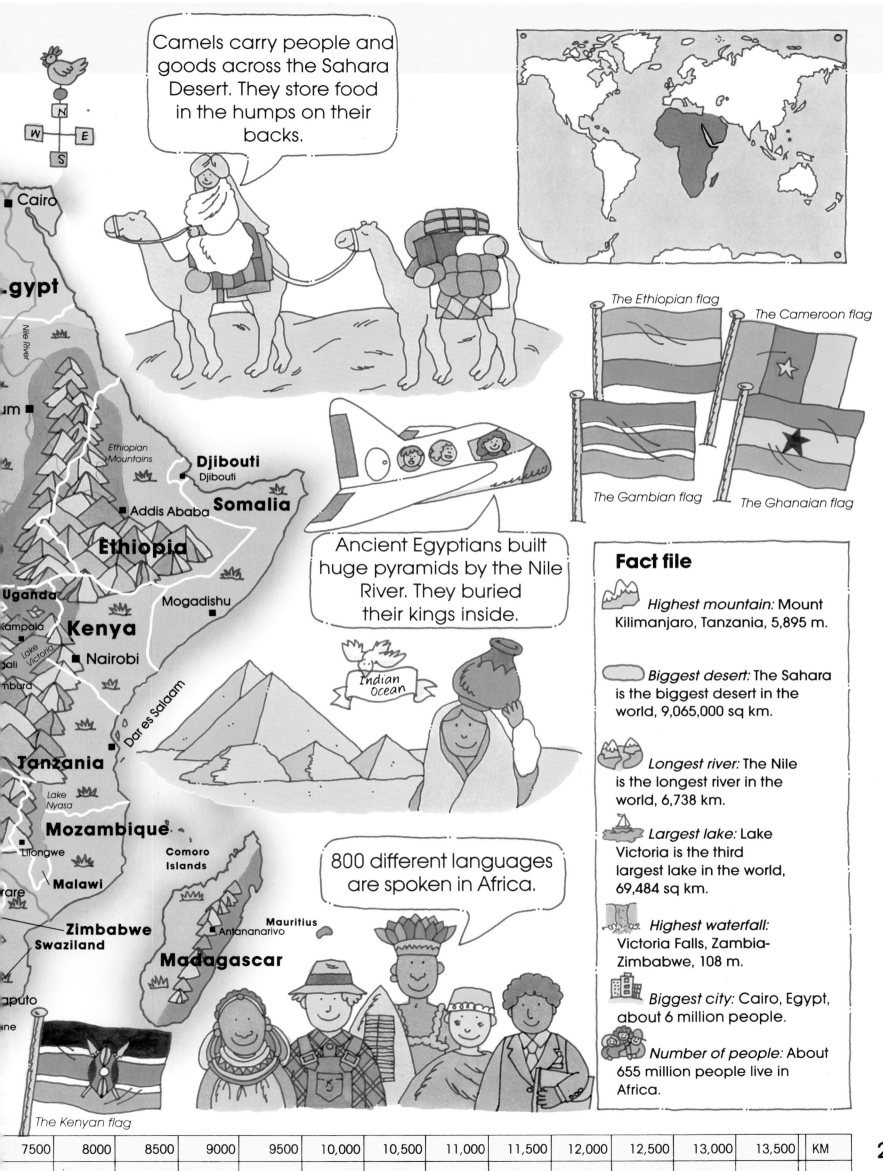

Camels carry people and goods across the Sahara Desert. They store food in the humps on their backs.

*The Ethiopian flag*

*The Cameroon flag*

*The Gambian flag*

*The Ghanaian flag*

■ Cairo

-gypt

*Nile River*

um ■

*Ethiopian Mountains*

**Djibouti**
Djibouti

■ Addis Ababa

**Somalia**

**Ethiopia**

**Uganda**

Mogadishu ■

**Kenya**

■ Nairobi

*Lake Victoria*

Ancient Egyptians built huge pyramids by the Nile River. They buried their kings inside.

*Indian Ocean*

Dar es Salaam

**Tanzania**

*Lake Nyasa*

**Mozambique**

Lilongwe

Comoro Islands

800 different languages are spoken in Africa.

**Malawi**

*Mauritius*
■ Antananarivo

**Zimbabwe**
**Swaziland**

**Madagascar**

aputo

ne

*The Kenyan flag*

## Fact file

*Highest mountain:* Mount Kilimanjaro, Tanzania, 5,895 m.

*Biggest desert:* The Sahara is the biggest desert in the world, 9,065,000 sq km.

*Longest river:* The Nile is the longest river in the world, 6,738 km.

*Largest lake:* Lake Victoria is the third largest lake in the world, 69,484 sq km.

*Highest waterfall:* Victoria Falls, Zambia-Zimbabwe, 108 m.

*Biggest city:* Cairo, Egypt, about 6 million people.

*Number of people:* About 655 million people live in Africa.

| 7500 | 8000 | 8500 | 9000 | 9500 | 10,000 | 10,500 | 11,000 | 11,500 | 12,000 | 12,500 | 13,000 | 13,500 | KM |
|------|------|------|------|------|--------|--------|--------|--------|--------|--------|--------|--------|-----|

# The Former U.S.S.R.

In 1991 the former U.S.S.R. (the Soviet Union) broke up into 15 separate republics. Estonia, Lithuania and Latvia became fully independent. Most of the other republics agreed to work together in a Commonwealth.

The north is freezing cold, but the deserts in the south are burning hot. In between there are forests and farmlands.

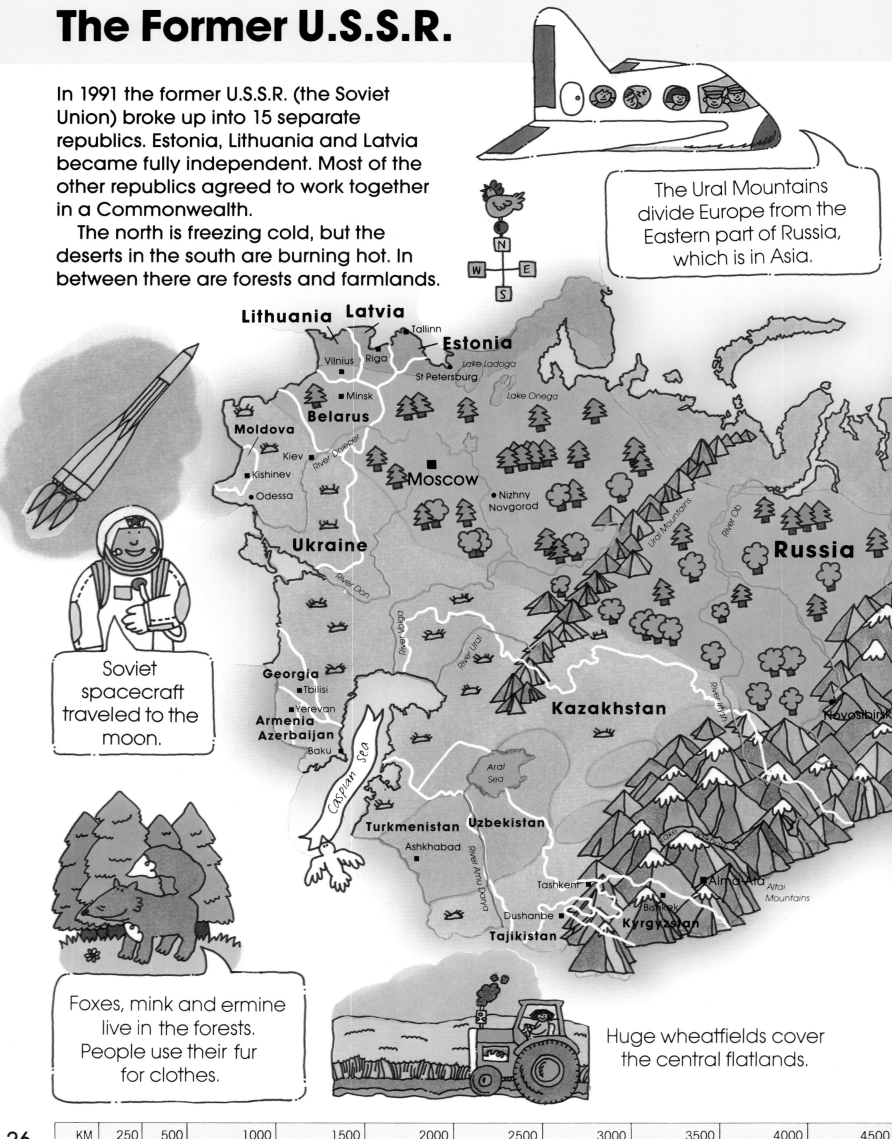

The Ural Mountains divide Europe from the Eastern part of Russia, which is in Asia.

Soviet spacecraft traveled to the moon.

Foxes, mink and ermine live in the forests. People use their fur for clothes.

Huge wheatfields cover the central flatlands.

Lithuania · Latvia · Estonia
Vilnius · Riga · Tallinn
Lake Ladoga · St Petersburg
Minsk · Lake Onega
Belarus
Moldova
Kiev · River Dnieper
Kishinev
Odessa
Moscow
Nizhny Novgorod
Ukraine
River Don
River Volga
River Ural
Ural Mountains
River Ob
Russia
Georgia
Tbilisi
Yerevan
Armenia
Azerbaijan
Baku
Caspian Sea
Aral Sea
Kazakhstan
River Irtysh
Novosibirsk
Turkmenistan
Ashkhabad
Uzbekistan
River Amu Darya
Tashkent
Lake Balkhash
Alma-Ata
Altai Mountains
Bishkek
Dushanbe
Kyrgyzstan
Tajikistan

| KM | 250 | 500 | 1000 | 1500 | 2000 | 2500 | 3000 | 3500 | 4000 | 4500 |
|----|-----|-----|------|------|------|------|------|------|------|------|
|    |     |     |      |      |      |      |      |      |      |      |

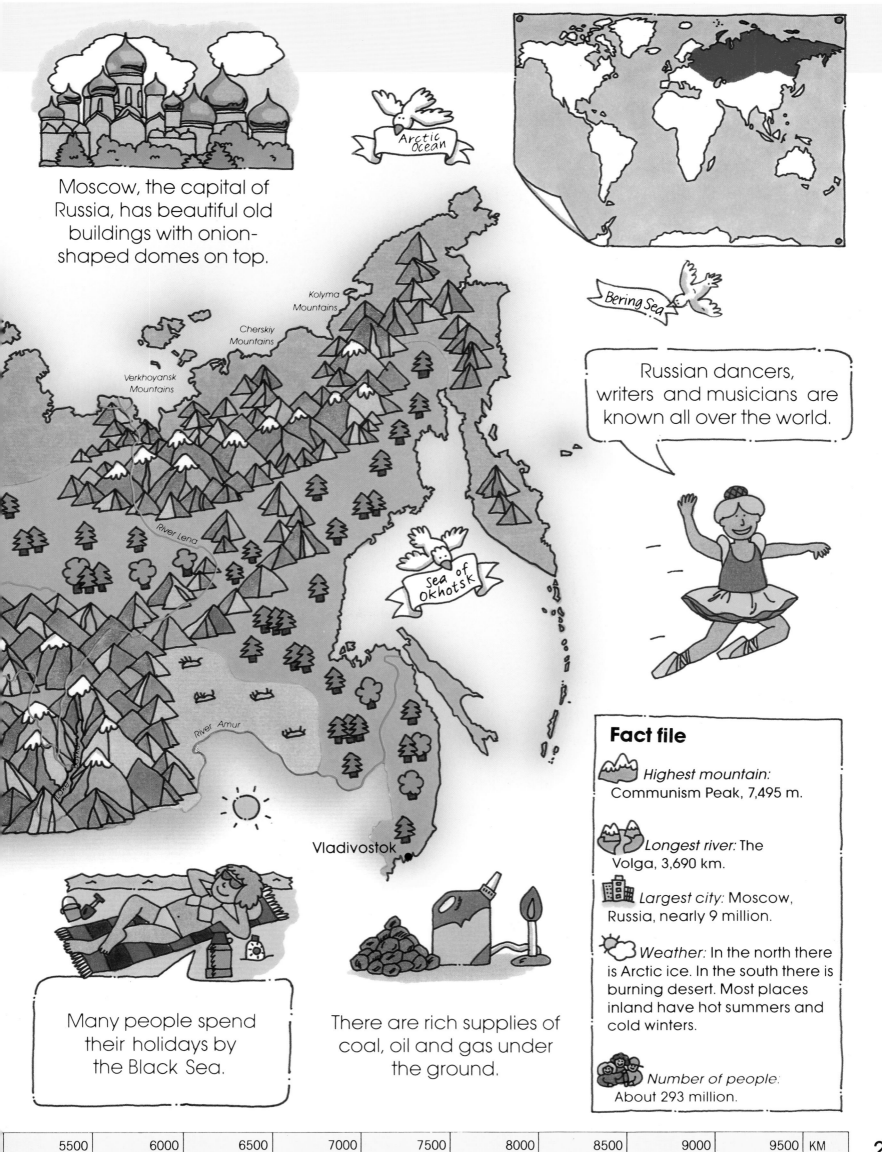

Moscow, the capital of Russia, has beautiful old buildings with onion-shaped domes on top.

Arctic Ocean

Bering Sea

Russian dancers, writers and musicians are known all over the world.

Kolyma Mountains

Cherskiy Mountains

Verkhoyansk Mountains

River Lena

Sea of Okhotsk

River Amur

Vladivostok

Many people spend their holidays by the Black Sea.

There are rich supplies of coal, oil and gas under the ground.

**Fact file**

*Highest mountain:* Communism Peak, 7,495 m.

*Longest river:* The Volga, 3,690 km.

*Largest city:* Moscow, Russia, nearly 9 million.

*Weather:* In the north there is Arctic ice. In the south there is burning desert. Most places inland have hot summers and cold winters.

*Number of people:* About 293 million.

| | 5500 | 6000 | 6500 | 7000 | 7500 | 8000 | 8500 | 9000 | 9500 | KM |
|---|---|---|---|---|---|---|---|---|---|---|

# The Middle East

Most of the Middle East is either mountainous or hot, sandy desert. Some of the countries have a great deal of valuable oil under the ground. The oil is pumped up to the surface at oil wells. It is then sold to other countries for use as gasoline and other kinds of fuel.

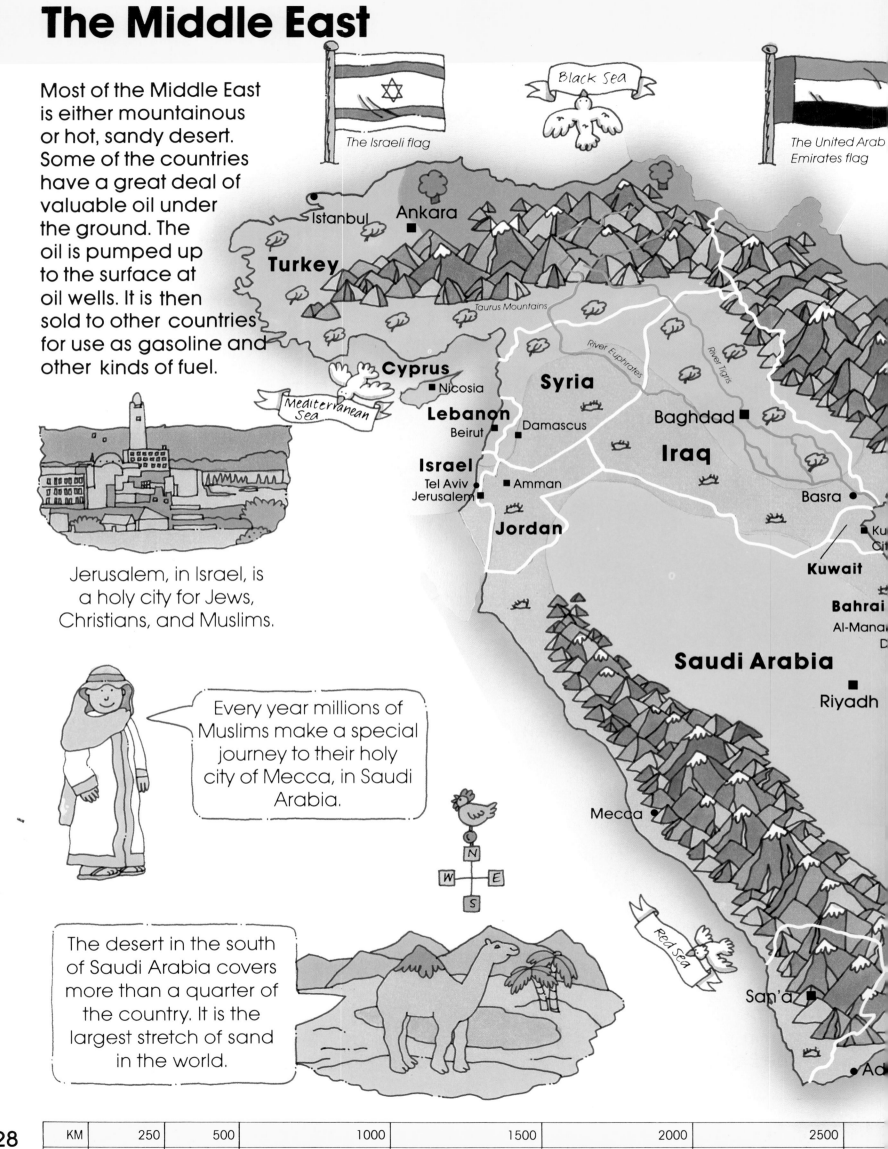

*The Israeli flag*

Black Sea

*The United Arab Emirates flag*

Istanbul
Ankara ■
**Turkey**

Taurus Mountains

River Euphrates
River Tigris

**Cyprus**
■ Nicosia

Mediterranean Sea

**Syria**

**Lebanon**
Beirut ■
Damascus ■

Baghdad ■

**Iraq**

**Israel**
Tel Aviv
Jerusalem ■
■ Amman

Basra ●

**Jordan**

Ku Cit

**Kuwait**

**Bahrai**
Al-Mana
D

**Saudi Arabia**

Riyadh ■

Jerusalem, in Israel, is a holy city for Jews, Christians, and Muslims.

Every year millions of Muslims make a special journey to their holy city of Mecca, in Saudi Arabia.

Mecca ●

N
W E
S

The desert in the south of Saudi Arabia covers more than a quarter of the country. It is the largest stretch of sand in the world.

Red Sea

San'a ■

● Ad

| KM | 250 | 500 | 1000 | 1500 | 2000 | 2500 |
|---|---|---|---|---|---|---|
| | | | | | | |

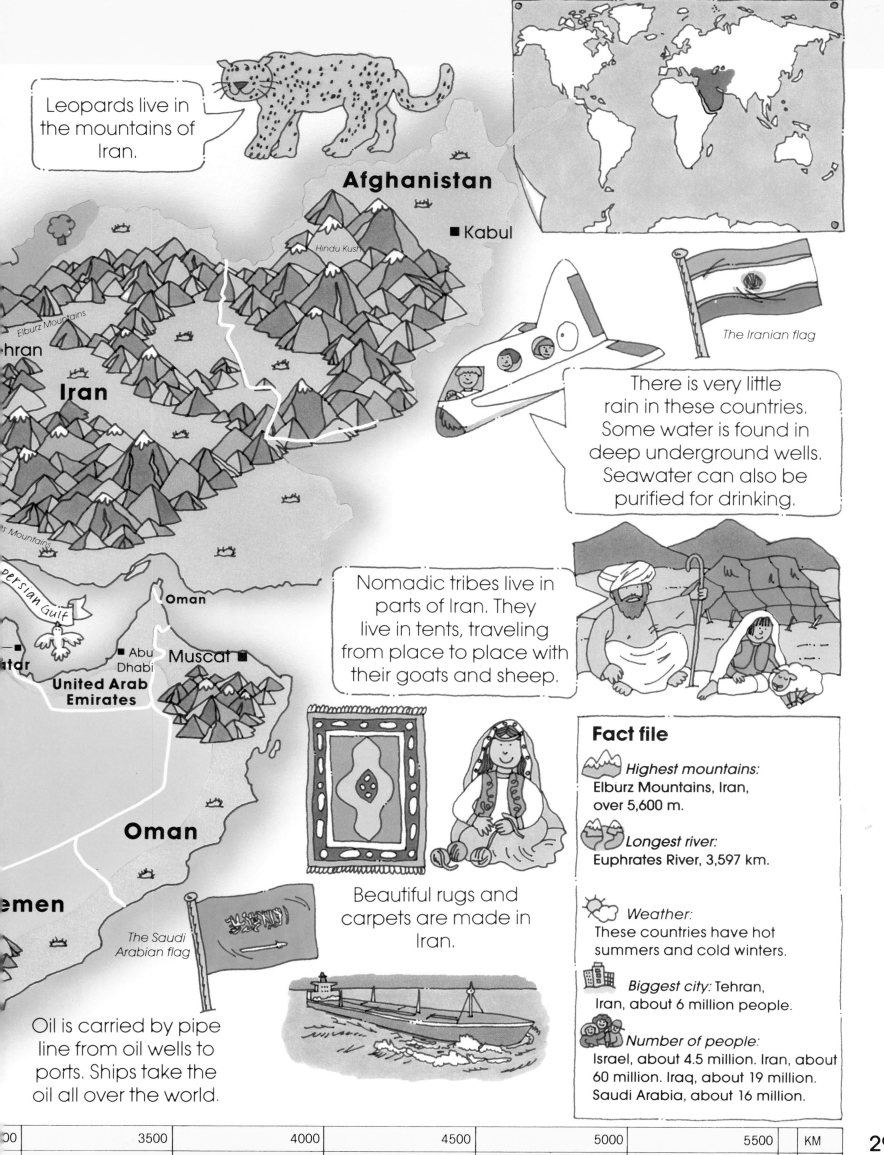

Leopards live in the mountains of Iran.

**Afghanistan**

Kabul

Hindu Kush

Elburz Mountains

hran

**Iran**

s Mountains

Persian Gulf

atar

**Oman**

Abu Dhabi

Muscat

**United Arab Emirates**

**Oman**

emen

The Saudi Arabian flag

Oil is carried by pipe line from oil wells to ports. Ships take the oil all over the world.

The Iranian flag

There is very little rain in these countries. Some water is found in deep underground wells. Seawater can also be purified for drinking.

Nomadic tribes live in parts of Iran. They live in tents, traveling from place to place with their goats and sheep.

Beautiful rugs and carpets are made in Iran.

**Fact file**

*Highest mountains:* Elburz Mountains, Iran, over 5,600 m.

*Longest river:* Euphrates River, 3,597 km.

*Weather:* These countries have hot summers and cold winters.

*Biggest city:* Tehran, Iran, about 6 million people.

*Number of people:* Israel, about 4.5 million. Iran, about 60 million. Iraq, about 19 million. Saudi Arabia, about 16 million.

| 00 | 3500 | 4000 | 4500 | 5000 | 5500 | KM |

# South Asia

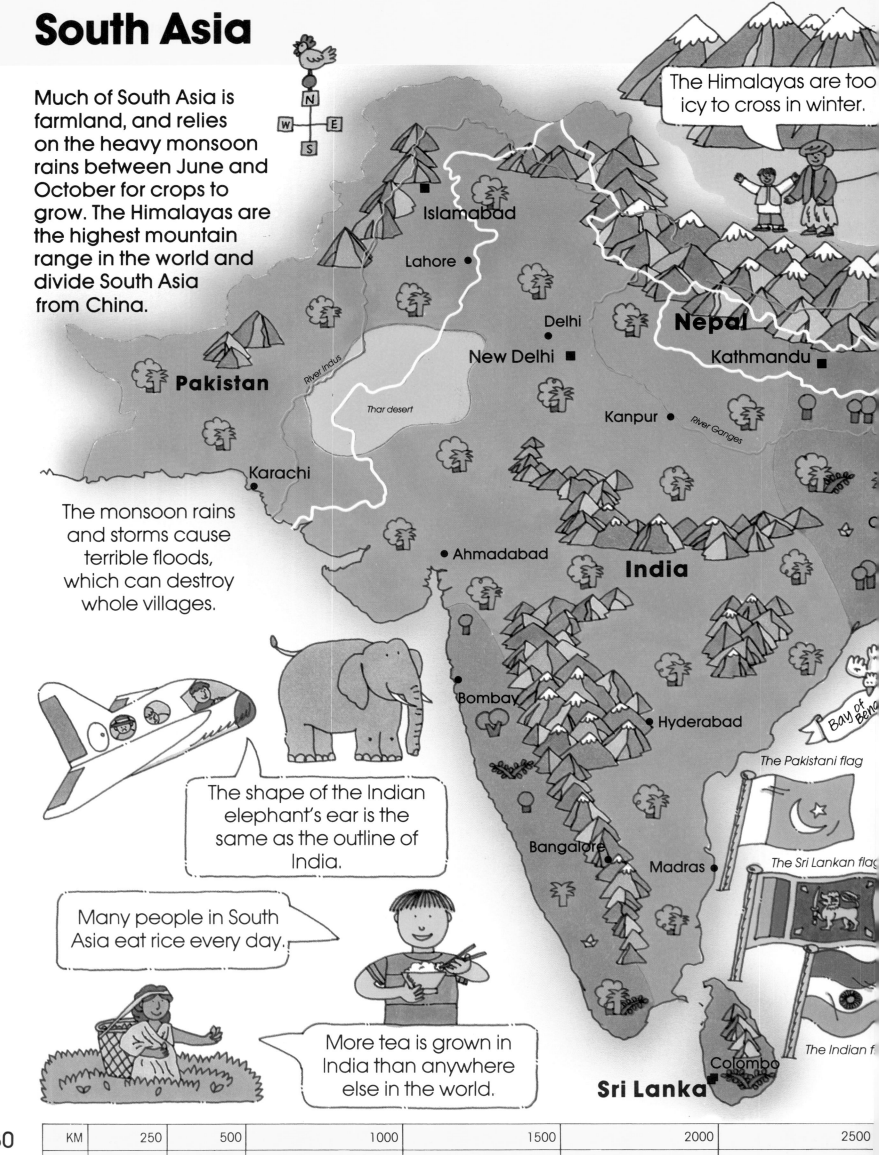

Much of South Asia is farmland, and relies on the heavy monsoon rains between June and October for crops to grow. The Himalayas are the highest mountain range in the world and divide South Asia from China.

The Himalayas are too icy to cross in winter.

The monsoon rains and storms cause terrible floods, which can destroy whole villages.

The shape of the Indian elephant's ear is the same as the outline of India.

Many people in South Asia eat rice every day.

More tea is grown in India than anywhere else in the world.

Islamabad

Lahore

Delhi

New Delhi

Nepal

Kathmandu

River Indus

Thar desert

Pakistan

Kanpur

River Ganges

Karachi

Ahmadabad

India

Bombay

Hyderabad

Bay of Bengal

The Pakistani flag

Bangalore

Madras

The Sri Lankan flag

The Indian f

Colombo

Sri Lanka

| KM | | 250 | 500 | | 1000 | | 1500 | | 2000 | | 2500 |

Ponies and yaks are used to carry goods across the Himalayas.

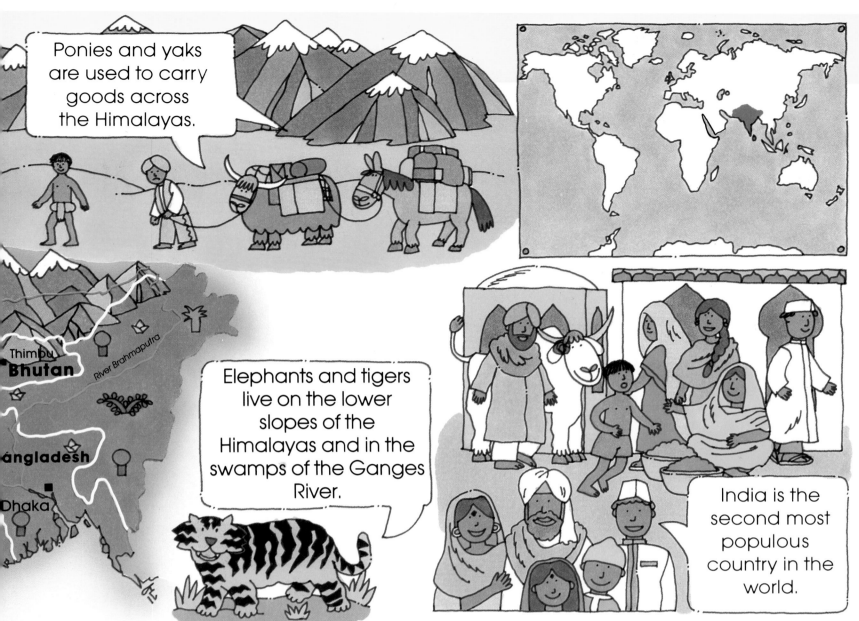

Thimbu
**Bhutan**
River Brahmaputra

**ngladesh**

Dhaka

Elephants and tigers live on the lower slopes of the Himalayas and in the swamps of the Ganges River.

India is the second most populous country in the world.

## Fact file

*Highest mountain:* Mount Everest, 8,848 m.

*Longest river:* Ganges-Brahmaputra, 2,900 km.

*Weather:* It is very cold in the mountains, but hot most of the year elsewhere.

*Biggest city:* Calcutta, India, about 11 million people.

*Number of people in some countries:*
Nepal, about 19 million.
Bangladesh, about 108 million.
Bhutan, about 600,000.
India, about 844 million.
Sri Lanka, about 17 million.
Pakistan, about 114 million.

Cows are sacred animals in India. They are not kept in fields but are allowed to graze where they like.

Cotton plants produce threads that are made into cotton fabric. It can be painted or dyed and made into clothes.

The Taj Mahal, near Agra in northern India, is often called the most beautiful building in the world.

# Southeast Asia

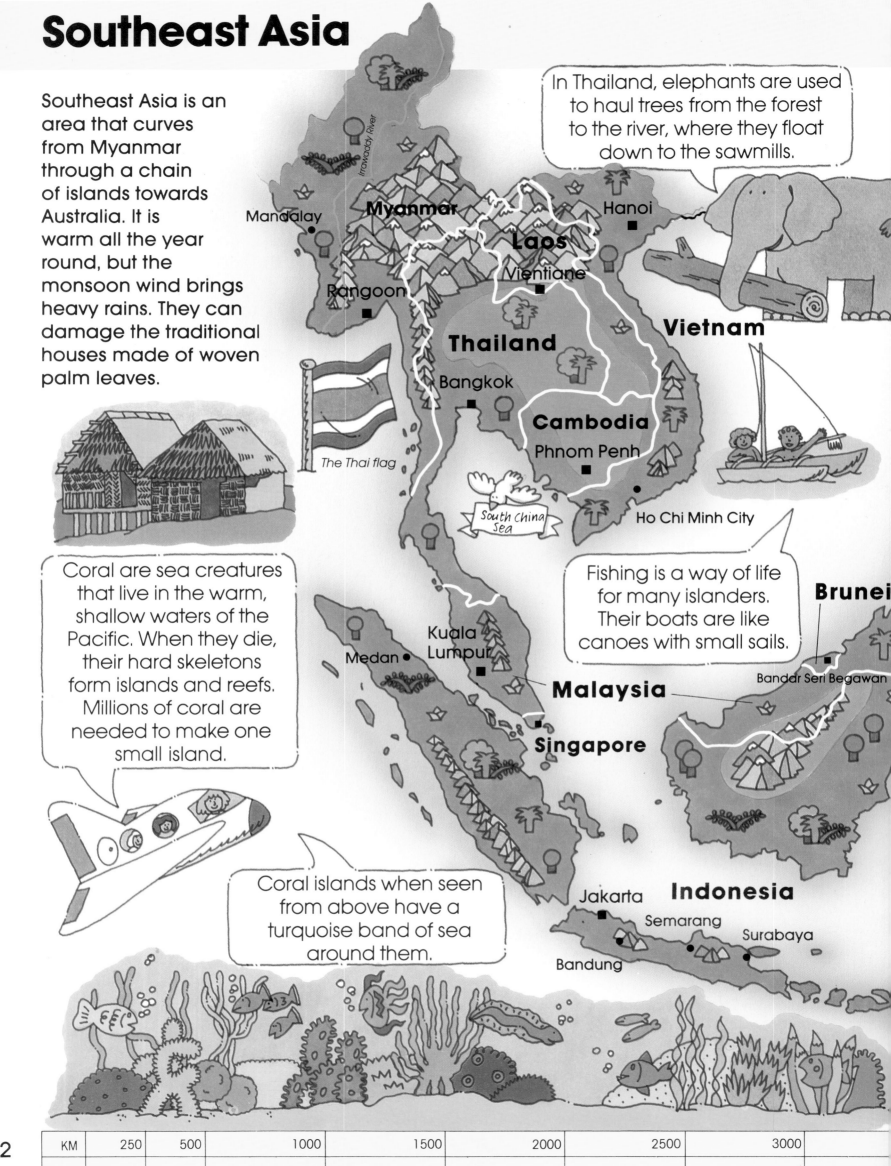

Southeast Asia is an area that curves from Myanmar through a chain of islands towards Australia. It is warm all the year round, but the monsoon wind brings heavy rains. They can damage the traditional houses made of woven palm leaves.

In Thailand, elephants are used to haul trees from the forest to the river, where they float down to the sawmills.

The Thai flag

Coral are sea creatures that live in the warm, shallow waters of the Pacific. When they die, their hard skeletons form islands and reefs. Millions of coral are needed to make one small island.

Fishing is a way of life for many islanders. Their boats are like canoes with small sails.

Coral islands when seen from above have a turquoise band of sea around them.

Irrawaddy River

Mandalay

Myanmar

Rangoon

Thailand

Bangkok

Laos

Vientiane

Hanoi

Vietnam

Cambodia

Phnom Penh

South China Sea

Ho Chi Minh City

Brunei

Bandar Seri Begawan

Medan

Kuala Lumpur

Malaysia

Singapore

Jakarta

Indonesia

Semarang

Surabaya

Bandung

| KM | 250 | 500 | | 1000 | | 1500 | | 2000 | | 2500 | | 3000 |
|---|---|---|---|---|---|---|---|---|---|---|---|---|
| | | | | | | | | | | | | |

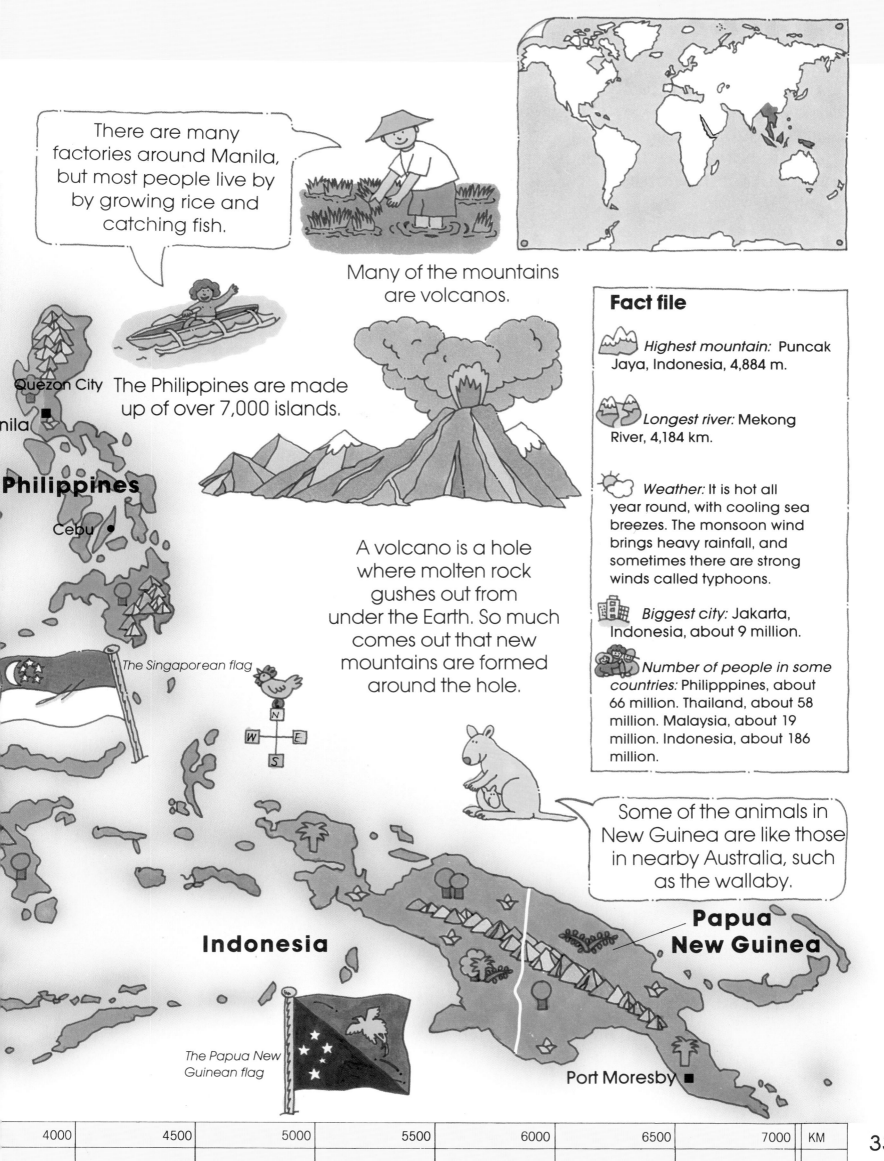

There are many factories around Manila, but most people live by by growing rice and catching fish.

Many of the mountains are volcanos.

The Philippines are made up of over 7,000 islands.

Quezon City

nila

**Philippines**

Cebu •

A volcano is a hole where molten rock gushes out from under the Earth. So much comes out that new mountains are formed around the hole.

*The Singaporean flag*

N
W E
S

**Fact file**

*Highest mountain:* Puncak Jaya, Indonesia, 4,884 m.

*Longest river:* Mekong River, 4,184 km.

*Weather:* It is hot all year round, with cooling sea breezes. The monsoon wind brings heavy rainfall, and sometimes there are strong winds called typhoons.

*Biggest city:* Jakarta, Indonesia, about 9 million.

*Number of people in some countries:* Philipppines, about 66 million. Thailand, about 58 million. Malaysia, about 19 million. Indonesia, about 186 million.

Some of the animals in New Guinea are like those in nearby Australia, such as the wallaby.

**Papua New Guinea**

**Indonesia**

*The Papua New Guinean flag*

Port Moresby ■

| 4000 | 4500 | 5000 | 5500 | 6000 | 6500 | 7000 | KM |

# East Asia

China is the third largest country in the world. Japan is much smaller, about the same size as Britain, but it is the richest country in Asia.

Chinese temples and pagodas have tiled roofs that curl up at the corners.

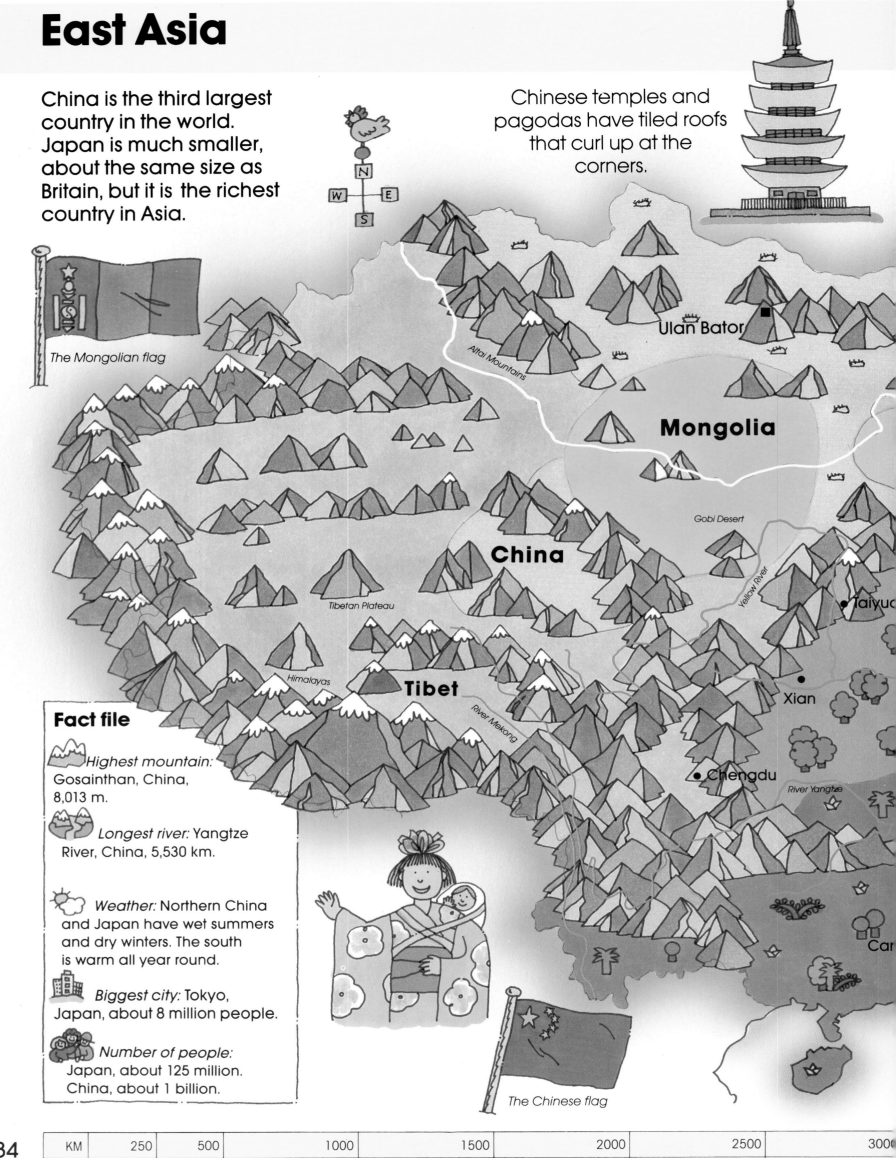

*The Mongolian flag*

N
W   E
S

Altai Mountains

Ulan Bator

**Mongolia**

Gobi Desert

Yellow River

**China**

Tibetan Plateau

Taiyua

Himalayas

**Tibet**

River Mekong

Xian

Chengdu

River Yangtze

Car

## Fact file

**Highest mountain:** Gosainthan, China, 8,013 m.

**Longest river:** Yangtze River, China, 5,530 km.

**Weather:** Northern China and Japan have wet summers and dry winters. The south is warm all year round.

**Biggest city:** Tokyo, Japan, about 8 million people.

**Number of people:** Japan, about 125 million. China, about 1 billion.

*The Chinese flag*

| KM | 250 | 500 | 1000 | 1500 | 2000 | 2500 | 300 |
|---|---|---|---|---|---|---|---|
| | | | | | | | |

Japan has many factories where people make cars, computers, and televisions.

*The Japanese flag*

River Amur

Harbin

Shen-yang

North Korea

Pyongyang

jing

Seoul

South Korea

Yellow Sea

Nanjing

Shanghai

The South Korean flag

Taipei

**Taiwan**
**Hong Kong**

The North Korean flag

Bears and a few giant pandas live in the southwest of China.

Sea of Japan

The ancient kingdom of Korea was divided into North and South Korea after the Second World War.

Tokyo

Hiroshima

Kyoto

**Japan**

Nagasaki

Pacific Ocean

The Great Wall of China was built over 2,000 years ago to keep out enemies. It winds 2,414 km across the hills of northern China.

Rice is grown in paddy fields. These are fields that are flooded by the rains or by rivers.

A fifth of the world's population lives in China.

# Australia and New Zealand

Australia is the smallest continent in the world. It lies in the southern Pacific Ocean, on the opposite side of the world from Europe. New Zealand is 1,500 km southeast of Australia. Most of Australia is flat and dry. New Zealand is more hilly and green.

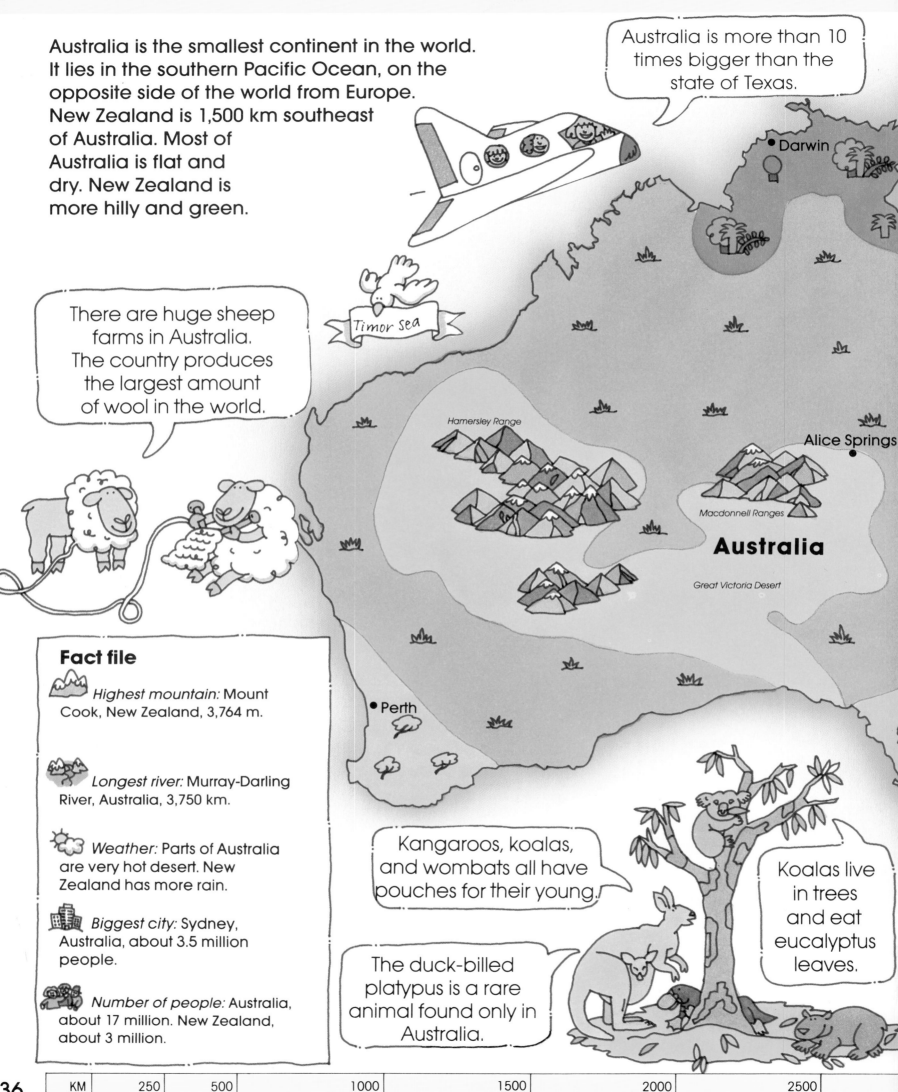

Australia is more than 10 times bigger than the state of Texas.

There are huge sheep farms in Australia. The country produces the largest amount of wool in the world.

Timor Sea

• Darwin

Hamersley Range

Alice Springs •

Macdonnell Ranges

**Australia**

Great Victoria Desert

• Perth

## Fact file

*Highest mountain:* Mount Cook, New Zealand, 3,764 m.

*Longest river:* Murray-Darling River, Australia, 3,750 km.

*Weather:* Parts of Australia are very hot desert. New Zealand has more rain.

*Biggest city:* Sydney, Australia, about 3.5 million people.

*Number of people:* Australia, about 17 million. New Zealand, about 3 million.

Kangaroos, koalas, and wombats all have pouches for their young.

Koalas live in trees and eat eucalyptus leaves.

The duck-billed platypus is a rare animal found only in Australia.

| KM | 250 | 500 | 1000 | 1500 | 2000 | 2500 |
|---|---|---|---|---|---|---|
| | | | | | | |

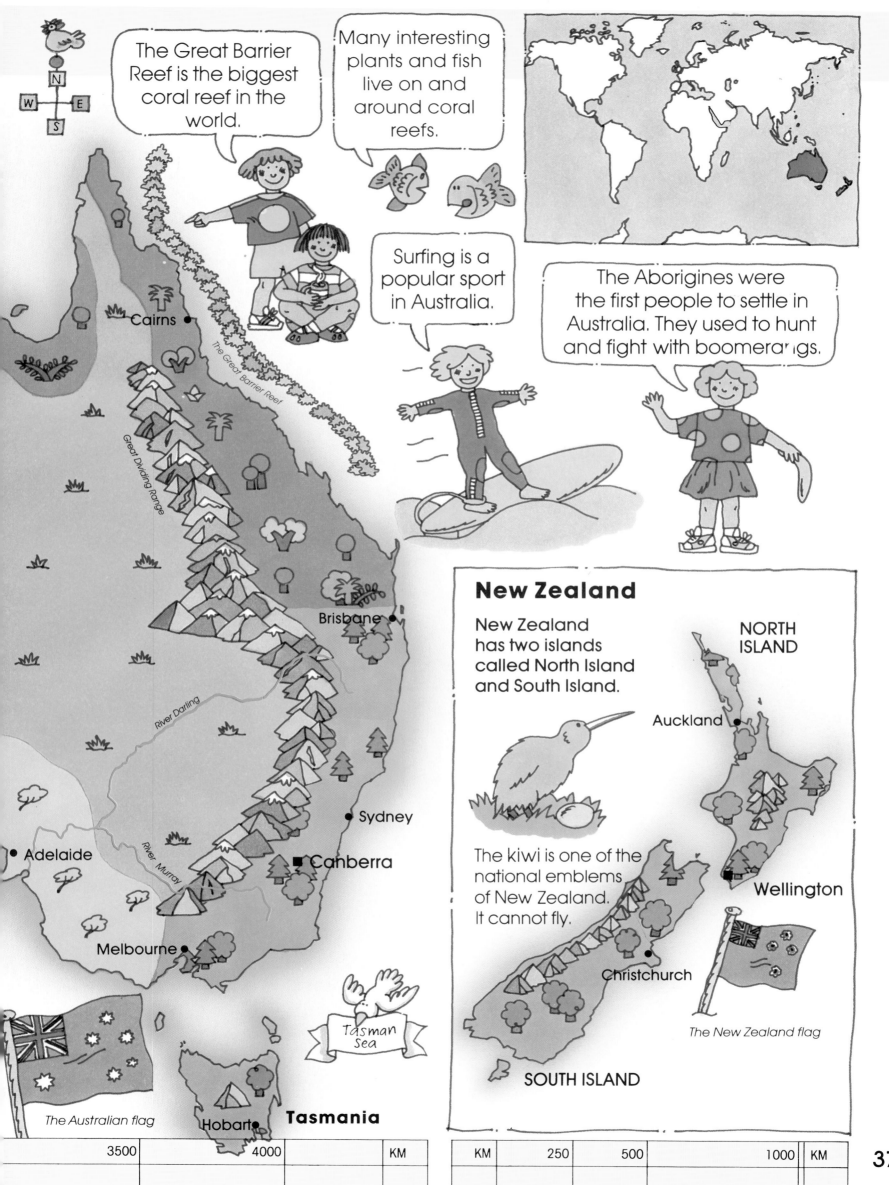

The Great Barrier Reef is the biggest coral reef in the world.

Many interesting plants and fish live on and around coral reefs.

Surfing is a popular sport in Australia.

The Aborigines were the first people to settle in Australia. They used to hunt and fight with boomerangs.

N
W E
S

Cairns

The Great Barrier Reef

Great Dividing Range

River Darling

River Murray

Adelaide

Brisbane

Sydney

Canberra

Melbourne

Tasman Sea

The Australian flag

Hobart

**Tasmania**

## New Zealand

New Zealand has two islands called North Island and South Island.

NORTH ISLAND

Auckland

The kiwi is one of the national emblems of New Zealand. It cannot fly.

Wellington

Christchurch

The New Zealand flag

SOUTH ISLAND

| | 3500 | | 4000 | | KM |
|---|---|---|---|---|---|

| KM | | 250 | 500 | | 1000 | KM |
|---|---|---|---|---|---|---|

# The Arctic

The Arctic is the area around the North Pole. It is frozen ocean surrounded by land. The ocean is covered with ice that slowly drifts from place to place.

*The Icelandic flag*

Polar bears live on the frozen sea. They catch seals to eat.

Alaska

Arctic Ocean

North Pole

Arctic Ocean

Canada

U.S.S.R.

Greenland

Sweden

Iceland

Arctic Circle

Finland

Norway

The Inuit live in the Arctic parts of Canada, Alaska, and Greenland.

In summer, most of the Arctic land is covered with plants. Grass and mosses grow there and many flowers bloom.

| KM | 250 | 500 | 1000 | 1500 | 2000 | 2500 | 3000 | 3500 | 4000 | 4500 | KM |
|---|---|---|---|---|---|---|---|---|---|---|---|
| | | | | | | | | | | | |

# The Antarctic

The Antarctic is ice-covered land around the South Pole. The ice is 4,500 meters thick in some places. There are many high mountains and some volcanos.

At the North and South Poles, winter and summer last six months each. Winter is dark all day and night. In summer it is light all the time.

The Arctic

The Antarctic

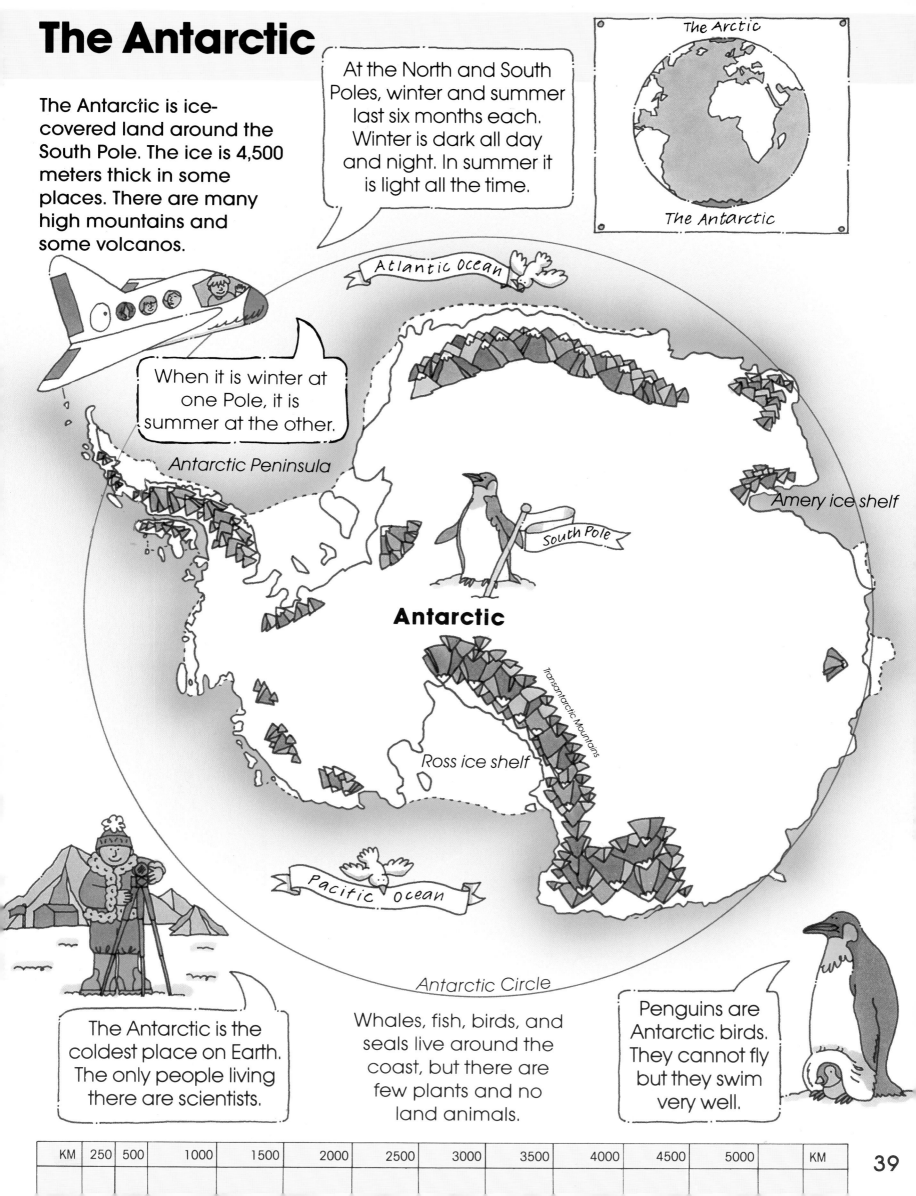

When it is winter at one Pole, it is summer at the other.

Atlantic Ocean

Antarctic Peninsula

Amery ice shelf

South Pole

**Antarctic**

Transantarctic Mountains

Ross ice shelf

Pacific Ocean

Antarctic Circle

The Antarctic is the coldest place on Earth. The only people living there are scientists.

Whales, fish, birds, and seals live around the coast, but there are few plants and no land animals.

Penguins are Antarctic birds. They cannot fly but they swim very well.

| KM | 250 | 500 | 1000 | 1500 | 2000 | 2500 | 3000 | 3500 | 4000 | 4500 | 5000 | KM |
|----|-----|-----|------|------|------|------|------|------|------|------|------|----|
|    |     |     |      |      |      |      |      |      |      |      |      |    |

# Index

This book was created and produced by Zigzag Publishing Ltd., The Barn, Randolph's Farm, Brighton Road, Hurstpierpoint, West Sussex, BN6 9EL

Map consultants: Sussex University Map Library
Geography consultant: Diane Snowden

Colour separations by RCS Graphics Ltd, Leeds.
Printed in Italy

Copyright © 1994 Zigzag Publishing Ltd.
This edition published by Whitecap Books Ltd.
351 Lynn Avenue, North Vancouver,
British Columbia V7J 2C4

Canadian Cataloguing in Publication Data

Main entry under title:
My first Canadian atlas

Includes index

ISBN 1-55110-253-6

1. Atlases, Canadian–Juvenile literature. 2. Canada–Maps–Juvenile literature. I. Potter, Tony
G1115.M9 1994      j912.71      C94-910422-1